1986

To Rick,

May you receive many blessings from the reading of this book, and share its wisdom with others—

Much love,
Janet & Morrie

D0455673

IF GOD CARES, WHY DO I STILL HAVE PROBLEMS?

Lloyd J. Ogilvie

IF GOD CARES, WHY DO I STILL HAVE PROBLEMS?

WORD BOOKS
PUBLISHER
WACO, TEXAS

A DIVISION OF
WORD, INCORPORATED

Library of Congress Cataloging in Publication Data

Ogilvie, Lloyd John.
  If God cares, why do I still have problems?

  1. Christian life—Presbyterian authors.
2. Providence and government of God. I. Title.
BV4501.2.O3293 1985   248.4'851   85–20296
ISBN 0–8499–0454–1

567898 FG   987654321

Printed in the United States of America

To
Dr. Richard Halverson
Chaplain of the United States Senate
Prophet and Pastor to the Nation
and
My Friend in Christ

CONTENTS

Introduction   9

1. If God Cares, Why Do I Still Have Problems?   15

2. When Problems Pile Up   28

3. Let Up, Ease Off, Let Go!   43

4. When Our Hearts Are Broken   56

5. The Law of Multiplying Returns   64

6. Losing Your Grip on Life   77

7. Freedom from Frustration   93

8. The Only Sure Cure for an Anxious Mind   108

9. Too Soon Old, Too Late Free   121

10. When We Feel Misunderstood   134

11. The Problem of Answered Prayer   150

12. When Life Kicks the Joy Out of You   165

13. People Problems   180

14. Handling Failures in the Victorious Christian Life   195

15. Beyond Our Doubts and Better Than Our Dreams   210

INTRODUCTION

WE'VE NICKNAMED HIM "No problem Harvey." He's one of the best waiters in Los Angeles. My wife and I enjoy going to the restaurant where he works. The food always tastes better when served by Harvey.

Whatever you ask of Harvey, his quick reply is "No problem!" He's anxious to please. The difficulty is that he says "No problem!" to whatever you say to him. As I got to know Harvey, I began to wonder if he knew that his constantly repeated, almost compulsive reply was said without thinking.

One evening I overheard from another table that the restaurant was out of one of the main entrees. So I decided to order that just to see what Harvey's answer would be.

"No problem!" he said, "We've been out of that for hours."

"Harvey," I asked warmly and with good humor, "why do you always say, 'No problem!' all the time even when there's a problem?"

"Do I always say that?" he asked, surprised. "I guess it's just a habit I picked up. I wish it was true—but we've all got problems. I sure got my share. Maybe I keep saying that so the problems will go away. Then maybe, knowing what problems can do to people, I don't want anything to be a problem when I serve them their meals. Whatever, no problem!"

I can identify with Harvey. In fact, for years I would have liked being called "No problem Lloyd." I didn't like problems. I didn't want to have problems and especially I didn't want to be a problem. Most of all, I wanted to solve other people's problems. Somewhere I picked up the idea that there was something inherently bad about problems.

Quite frankly, problems used to be an embarrassment to me. I thought that if I believed in God, said my prayers, and trusted Him with my needs, I should be free of problems. And yet, problems persisted. As a Christian leader I falsely felt that I should exemplify a problem-free life. Still, I had my share of problems. So I adopted the idea that I should try to model a victorious faith that confronted and solved problems courageously. I wrestled with my problems thinking that if only I had more faith, or tried harder, I'd finally reach a point when all of life's problems were behind me.

Of course, I never reached that point. At the same time, my negative attitude toward problems and my desire to keep up a front of a life without problems, made it difficult to talk about my problems. Even when it wasn't true my attitude communicated, "No problem!"

A deeper cause of that was that I assumed a responsibility for protecting God's reputation! What kind of God did I have to communicate to others if I still had problems? Either there was something lacking in me or God wasn't able to pull off the problem-free life I had mistakenly thought was a sign of His blessing. The latter of those two alternatives was not a possibility in my mind, so there must have been something wrong with my life that I wasn't able to rid myself of problems.

At the same time, I listened to people tell me about their problems. Many of them were Christians. Some of their problems were obviously caused by their own mistakes or failures. But what about the problems caused by other people or difficult circumstances? Why did God allow these distressing problems? I found people in the same dilemma as I was in. Either they didn't deserve God's blessing in the release from all their problems or He was not really concerned about their troublesome problems.

For years, I heard the same question. It was worded in many different ways but the frustration expressed was the same. "If God cares, why do I still have problems?" Problems were perceived of as either punishment for past failures, the absence of God, or the mischief of Satan.

What I and most of these people lacked was not faith but a profound understanding of the creative use and redemptive purpose of problems. Greater than any problem we face is the bigger problem of our confused thinking about problems!

That led me to a prolonged period of study and prayer about how God sometimes allows, and always uses, our problems for our growth and His glory. The greatest problem we all share, to a greater or lesser degree, is a profound misunderstanding of the positive purpose of problems. Until we grapple with this gigantic problem, we will be helpless victims of our problems all through our lives.

The conclusion I came to in my thinking about problems brought me to one of the most liberating discoveries of my life—and to the theme of this book. It is because God cares that we still have problems!

Does that unsettle you? It did me when I first began to wrestle with it. And yet, the more I have thought and prayed about it, the more it has released me to face my problems and trust the Lord to help me grow through them. And when one problem has passed, I know it's time to get ready for the next one. Instead of trying to avoid problems or pretending they don't exist, we can greet them as potential blessings. When the Lord allows a problem to surface, it is because He's ready to do a great work in us, in the people around us, or in our circumstances. A problem honestly confronted and accepted, surrendered to the Lord, and placed at His disposal for what He wants to teach us or change in us or our relationships, will become a source of deeper fellowship with Him, and an opportunity for our growth in greatness.

I want to spell out this life-changing conviction in the chapters of this book. To do that I plan to show how it works in the most distressing problems we all face.

In preparation for writing this book, I asked my congregation and our national television viewers to write me what they thought were the biggest problems we face in living today. The thousands of responses were sorted and put into categories of types of problems. Then I searched through the Bible for God's answers to these pressing problems. That led to another equally liberating discovery—not only does God have a redemptive purpose for problems, but He gives us a specific promise in the Bible for every problem. The focus of this book emerged: our problems and the promises of God.

From all the biggest problems people shared with me I selected those which seemed to be most disturbing to the greatest number of people. Each chapter deals with one of these and then explains the promise which is perfectly suited for that problem. My purpose is to show how that promise works in our life today as a part of the amazing way God uses problems. I can't wait to discuss with you all the implications of what I've discovered and what a difference it's made for my daily living.

I pray that you will sense what I felt as I wrote these chapters. For me, it was like a deep conversation between trusting friends. That's how I think of our relationship—not just author and reader—but as friends who really care about each other and can share not only our problems but can help each other discover God's plan, purpose and power through them.

Speaking of gratitude for friends, I want to express my profound thanks to all the people who made this book possible.

Thanks to the members of my beloved congregation, the

First Presbyterian Church of Hollywood, who shared their problems and the adventure of living out the secret the Lord gave us about getting the most out of them. And thanks to the growing family of faith partners across the nation who encourage our television ministry with their prayers and support. Many of the thoughts expressed in this book were a part of my weekly messages to them.

I am very thankful to God for the gift of friendship with Floyd Thatcher, Editor-in-Chief of Word Books. He was of immeasurable help in editing the manuscript and enabled me to communicate more clearly and precisely what I wanted to say in this book. His enthusiasm for the book spurred me on through several revisions.

Also I want to express my debt of gratitude to Pat Wienandt of Word who supervised the final editing and preparation for publication. It is always a joy to work with Pat and to receive her deep theological insight and marvelously helpful suggestions. Special thanks to Sheri Livingston for her invaluable help in readying the manuscript for the printer and planning interior design features.

Jerlyn Gonzalez, my administrative assistant, carefully read and reread the manuscript through its several stages and managed all the details to make its publication possible. I am thankful to her for her encouragement of the project from start to finish. And to Christina Hemme goes special thanks for typing my almost illegible handwritten chapters and then retyping them through many revisions.

To all these friends, I want to say thanks. No author has a finer team to work with and I can't imagine any who is more thankful than I am.

Now let's press on to discover together God's creative use and redemptive purpose of problems.

1

IF GOD CARES, WHY DO I STILL HAVE PROBLEMS?

"I WANT TO REGISTER a major complaint!" Sandy said as he opened our luncheon conversation.

Inside I groaned. I wondered what criticism my outspoken friend was about to level at me or the church.

"Don't look so defensive," he added quickly. "My quarrel isn't with you."

"Okay, then, what's the problem?"

"That's what I want to talk about. Problems! I've got more than my share right now—more than I deserve. I believe in God, say my prayers, live a decent life, but I've still got problems.

"What I want to know is if He is so kind and caring, why doesn't He distribute problems with more fairness? When I became a Christian, I thought that would be the end of my problems.

"But I've got as many as I've ever had. Why become a Christian if it doesn't assure us of freedom from problems? Sorry to complain, but I really feel God has let me down!"

Ever feel that way? Of course, we all have.

Sandy was asking the profound question that I hear everywhere these days: If God cares, why do I still have problems? I hear it from young and old, the rich and poor, church members and secular Americans alike. It seems that people who are successful in one area of life still have problems in other areas. I've also talked with people who have zoomed through life with relative ease, but then without any warning they are suddenly overwhelmed with problems. And there are those who seem to be struggling with problems at every stage of life. Why does God allow good people—serious Christians—to have problems?

Our Biggest Problem

Years of wrestling with my own problems, and trying to help people endure their own, have convinced me of a fact of life. We all face one great problem that's bigger than all of the others.

Now having said that and before I tell you what I think that problem is, I want you to stop a moment and reflect on what you believe is your biggest problem. Unless I miss my guess, your thinking will focus either on some difficult person, or on a strained or broken relationship, or on some complex and seemingly impossible situation, or on some emotional pain or physical pain that's plaguing you right now.

When I asked people in my church and our national television viewers to write and tell me what they believed to be their biggest problem, the answers were not the least bit surprising. One way or another, all of the problems listed were common to all of us. And yet as I studied them, I came to feel that everything mentioned was dwarfed by the one momentous problem that cripples us as we attempt to handle all of our lesser ones.

Let me tell you what I've come to believe is this "one momentous problem." It's our failure to understand that there is a positive and redemptive purpose to every one of the problems we face. It is this deep truth that completely changed my attitude, and I've come to feel that until we confront that problem, we will be helpless victims of problems all through our lives.

Three Causes of Our Biggest Problem

Ingrained in our thinking are three false ideas about problems. And it is these, I believe, that cause us to miss the creative purpose of problems.

False Idea #1. We believe that there is something inherently bad about problems because they often involve us in unpleasant pressures, distressing conflict, or in an inconvenient interruption of our plans for a smooth and easy life. We conclude that problems are bad for us. We all like things to remain pleasant, successful, and satisfying. We think of problems as a bother, a distraction from our carefully laid plans, and an invasion of what we think makes us happy.

False Idea #2. We think that freedom from problems should be a reward for hard work, careful planning, and clear thinking. Present within each of us is the fond hope that out ahead somewhere, sometime, our life will be free of problems of any kind.

We struggle through the stages of life, battling the problems of getting an education, finding a job, developing a career, raising a family, making ends meet, and eventually retiring. At each stage we look forward to the next period as a time when the problems of life will be behind us.

We think we can take most any problem if we are assured that eventually the period of problems will end. Then, when we finally achieve the success we've been working for, or finish some problem-filled project, or reach our goal of financial security, we are alarmed and discouraged when there are still problems that hassle us.

As one woman put it, "My husband and I have had more

than our share of problems all through the years. We kept thinking the struggle was worth it because someday we'd get to a place when all our problems would be solved. Now look at us. We've arrived at where we wanted to be financially and socially, and we've still got problems! Yes, they're different problems, but they are no less distressing. When will the problems of life ever go away?"

False Idea #3. We think that if we love God, commit our lives to Him, and diligently try to serve Him, He will work things out for us so everything will run smoothly and we'll be free from problems. But when it doesn't work that way, we ask, "Why should this happen to me?" Most serious of all, we begin to question the Lord's love for us. Somehow we see ourselves as His darlings who should be treated differently from everyone else.

We find it easy to understand why unbelievers or scoundrels have problems, but inevitably we ask, "Why does a just and loving God permit Christians like us to experience difficulties and hard times?" We're always ready to accept and praise Him for our blessings, but we fail to see that so often our problems are really blessings in disguise. And because of this failure, resentment and self-pity set in. We feel God cannot love us or care about us if He allows problems. But, the problems don't seem to go away. We end up with them and a strained relationship with God because He allowed the problems to happen. We back ourselves into a corner from which there seems to be no escape.

And when problems persist, we feel someone or something must be blamed—ourselves, others, circumstances, the mysterious force of evil undeniably rampant in the world, even God.

Our idea that there could never be any good to be gained out of problems causes us great difficulty. It spins us around in a spiraling cycle of thinking that eventually prompts us to confront God and question Him about His reward system. "God, don't You know that problems hurt and hinder me? What are You doing about my problems?"

If and Why

All this leads to what I call the impertinent "if" and the imperious "why." If *God loves me,* why *do I still face problems?* We've all asked that and longed for an answer. Perhaps it's your most urgent question right now. Or when people around you ask the question, you realize you don't have an adequate answer for them or for yourself.

In casting about for an answer, sometimes we find even deeper questions lurking beneath the surface. *Is God really concerned about the problems we face? Can or will He do anything to help? Has He left or forsaken us? Are problems His way of punishing us?*

And then we ask ourselves the flip side of all these questions. *If I really clean up my act, will God step in to bless me with solutions to all my present problems and head off all my future problems?* Finally comes the most unsettling question of all: *Would a problem-free life be the most loving and creative gift God could give me?*

An Entirely Different Perspective on Problems

All of these questions eventually lead us to a thoughtful consideration of problems. As we leaf through the pages of the Bible, examine the experiences of its heroes and heroines, and then honestly review the lives of the truly great people of history, we are confronted with a truth which contradicts the three false ideas we talked about. All of these people had problems.

Then as we honestly reflect on our own experiences, a rather shocking truth emerges. Our greatest discoveries and our most significant progress toward maturity have come during those times in our lives when we have creatively worked through our problems. A problem-free life, we conclude, may not be the best of lives after all. God's blessing really can't be equated with an exemption from problems.

As I have wrestled with this dilemma in my own life, I

have come to see that *it is because God cares that we still have problems!*

Does that alarm you? It did me when I first began to grapple with it. And yet, the more I have prayed about that conviction and lived it out in the endless flow of problems I've had since, the Lord has helped me to live joyously in the midst of problems and get the best from them. In the remaining part of this chapter I'm going to share with you the process of thinking and praying which has led me to this liberating view of problems.

Problems Don't Happen without God's Permission

God's purposes are not thwarted by our problems. He is in charge and no problem is too big for Him. In fact, a careful study of history indicates that He works out His plan through the problems He allows in our lives. God is not the helpless victim of the problems we bring on ourselves, those caused by other people, or those that are the mischief of the force of evil in the world.

God gave us the awesome gift of freedom so that we could choose to love, glorify, and serve Him. The refusal to do that is the cause of many of the problems we bring on ourselves and is often the cause of problems we face with others. Humankind's rebellion is often collusive in social evil, injustice, and suffering.

We live in a world fallen from God's original purpose. And yet He never gives up on us. He intervenes in our lives, reveals His loving and forgiving heart, and uses the problems we face. In fact, God uses them to get our attention and to force us to realize we can't make it on our own. And He draws us into a deeper relationship with Him as we learn to trust Him for strength to cope with and overcome our problems.

The bracing truth is that no problem can happen without God's permission. And what He allows is always for a greater blessing than we could ever realize if we had no problems.

He is a mighty, all-powerful Lord who wants us to grow in His nature, grace, and power. And one of the ways He has elected to do that is through the problems we confront. Just as He created us in the beginning, so too He is the continuing creator Who is at work in us and our world.

Actually, problems define the battle line of the Lord's transforming encounter with ignorance, pride, selfishness, laziness, and resistance to growth in all of us. Problems often motivate us to reach out to Him for help in dealing with our insensitivity, greed, and injustice in our relationships and in society.

We can be certain that when God allows a problem, it is because He wants us to grow as persons. And when the problem is with another person, we can know there is something He is seeking to accomplish in that relationship. But of this we can be sure—God never gives us more than we can take. And with each problem He seeks a new step for us to take in becoming truly dynamic people.

Problems Are a Gift

When viewed in this light, we can affirm that our problems are a gift. And we can be thankful that the Lord considers us worthy to be cooperative agents in the forward movement of His redemptive plan. For it is as we face our problems and endeavor to discover what He is trying to say to us through each of them that we will discover the secret of true joy. And that joy is the outward result of His gift of His grace at work in us.

Problems indeed become a gift as we trust the Lord to help us with them. It is then that we are able to receive His gracious reshaping of our personalities and experience the depth of His care.

Problems Are a Sign We're Alive

The good news for all of us then is that problems are a vital life sign. Anyone unrealistic enough to claim not to have problems has begun to die spiritually and emotionally, and the time of physical death may be greatly accelerated. Such being the case, instead of trying to avoid problems, we should greet them as potential blessings. We can be sure of this—a problem honestly faced and accepted and surrendered to the Lord can be the means of drawing us into deeper fellowship with Him.

The Lord is constantly pressing ahead in the confrontation of anything in us, others, or our society which contradicts His plan and purpose for us. In perfectly timed, carefully orchestrated providence, He allows problems to perk to the surface. He doesn't send them. There are enough to go around already. But, according to His plan, He allows them to emerge because He is ready to deal with them through us.

Therefore, people who have problems are blessed indeed! The Lord has decided not to leave us as we are. He has willed to change things which debilitate our love for Him and our love for the people in our lives. He's on the move calling us into social battles for truth and righteousness. So, in reality, a good test of how alive we are is in how many soul-sized problems the Lord has allowed us to tackle with His power and guidance.

Problems and Promises

It is in each problem that we discover a perfectly matched promise from God of what He will do to help us. Recently I made a list of the thousands of problems people sent me in response to my survey. Then I went through the Bible and underlined the direct quotes of promises from God in the Old Testament and those made through Christ in the New Testament. I could not find one problem for which there was not a promise uniquely suited to help us face and conquer it.

We can take encouragement in the fact that times of problems give us the opportunity to understand, claim, and experience these promises of God. Keats was right: "Nothing becomes real till it is experienced—even a proverb is no prov- erb to you till your life has illustrated it. . . . Call the world if you please, 'The vale of soul-making.' " The truth of God's promises is discovered and realized in our personal growth in the "vale of soul-making" forced upon us by our problems. In this book we will illustrate how the promises of God give us courage to receive the full potential for growth in all of our problems.

The Lord Never Leaves or Forsakes Us

While there is much in life we can't be sure of, God's Word trumpets a truth we can count on—irrespective of the intensity of our problems, the Lord of all creation is with us. In fact, our problems are proof of the presence of the recreating Lord, not His absence. And the bigger the problem, the more of His abiding presence we will receive. The more complex the problem, the more advanced will be the wisdom He offers. Equal to the strain of the problem will be the strength that is released. It is an evidence of the Lord's presence with us when He allows problems to focus the next step of what He wants to accomplish in our personal lives or through us in the lives of others, in the church, or in our society.

The Gideon in All of Us

This is the momentous discovery made by Gideon at a very difficult time of problems in Israel. As happens to us so often, the young Israelite had fallen into the trap of thinking that the presence of problems was an indication that the Lord wasn't with him.

But to understand the Gideon story we need to move back in history to the time when the people of Israel finally took God at His word and dared to cross over the Jordan River and possess the promised land of Canaan. After their years of wandering in the Sinai wilderness they were ill prepared for the rigors of agricultural life. In their attempt to succeed, they blended their worship of God with worship of the fertility Baal gods. Shrines for Baal and Asherah were placed in their fields to insure a good harvest. But these pagan rites, borrowed from their neighbors, did not bring them the prosperity they desired. Life was beset with problems. And then to complicate their problems, the Midianites and Amalekites would attack them at harvest time and carry off their grain and cattle. The Israelites were never out of danger.

Meanwhile the leaders of Israel remembered and recounted the mighty acts of God on their behalf during the Exodus. So, when God did not act in that way on their behalf when they faced problems in Canaan, they decided He no longer cared about their plight and had deserted them. Never once did it occur to them that it was their worship of the pagan god Baal that blocked the Lord from acting on their behalf. Their problem wasn't the hostile Midianites and Amalekites. Rather, their problems resulted from their own lack of trust in the Lord. God had not left His people; they had turned away from Him.

Our first introduction to Gideon (Judg. 6) finds him threshing out his meager wheat crop inside a winepress in a glen instead of on a threshing floor up near the fields, out in the open. We picture him at work, furtively flailing the wheat, cautiously looking around, anticipating an enemy attack at any moment. A sense of futility grips him as he thinks about his problems and wonders why the Lord does not step in to help him and his people. Gideon's anxious mood is not prepared for an encounter with the very Lord he felt had deserted His people.

That's how it often happens. At the lowest ebb of our endurance, when problems have gotten the best of us and we feel the Lord has forgotten and forsaken us, He breaks through with an assurance of His presence.

For Gideon, the transforming encounter began with an angel of the Lord and then with the Lord Himself. The angel astounded the beleaguered, problem-burdened Israelite with the awesome words, "The Lord is with you, you mighty man of valor!"

What an amazing contradiction that seems to be! A man of valor? Hiding in a winepress? And how could the Lord be with him when he had such momentous problems?

Gideon's response to the angel reveals his mood and frame of mind. Paraphrased, it is really our question, "If God cares, why do I still have problems?"

Out of the burning cauldron of Gideon's problem-filled life comes what seems to be a blatant blasphemy. "O my lord," he protested, "if the Lord is with us, why then has all this happened to us? And where *are* all His miracles which our fathers told us about, saying, 'Did not the Lord bring us up from Egypt?' But now the Lord has forsaken us and delivered us into the hands of the Midianites" (Judg. 6:13). We can see from this that he equated God's blessing only with miracles.

But God was patient with Gideon's false perceptions and questions. He called him to be a cooperative agent in the resolution of the very problems the frightened man had blamed on what he thought was His absence: "Go in this might of yours, and you shall save Israel from the hand of the Midianites" (v. 14).

How thankful we can be that the Lord doesn't give up on us. Instead He uses the problems we face to call us back to Him and then involves us in the solution He has planned.

Next we see that in response to the Lord's orders, Gideon's question shifts from his concern over why the Lord allowed the problem. Now, he questions his own ability to handle the challenge the Lord just gave him, "O my Lord, how can I save Israel? Indeed, my clan is the weakest in Manasseh, and I am the least in my father's house" (v. 15). How quickly Gideon's criticism of the Lord dissolved when he discovered that he was to be part of the solution to the problem!

It was then that God offered Gideon a promise that was equal to his problem. "Surely I will be with you, and you shall defeat Midian as one man" (v. 16). With these words Gideon knew that the Lord would be his strength, courage, and ultimate victory over his enemies.

Before leaving this part of the Gideon story I want to share an interesting insight. The first words the angel spoke to Gideon as translated in the Septuagint version of the Old Testament were "The Lord is with you, even the Lord in valor," or "The Lord is with you, *the* mighty Man of Valor." It was the Lord, not Gideon, who would be the source of his valor. The previously fearful man would become a great liberator of his people because his courage would be a gift from the intervening Lord.

Judges, chapters six through eight, gives us the rest of the story. The Lord convinced Gideon of His presence by bringing fire to consume a sacrifice he offered under the terebinth tree. He gave Gideon the courage to begin a reformation in Israel's religious life by tearing down the Baal shrine in his own fields.

When Gideon confessed his lack of strength, the Lord filled him with His Spirit and gave him the daring to call Israel to arms. Next, the Lord fulfilled Gideon's fleece test to convince him that He would be faithful to His promise. Then to be sure his trust was in Him and not in his army the Lord reduced the number of Gideon's soldiers from thirty-two thousand to three hundred faithful men.

To further overcome Gideon's fears, the Lord arranged for him to overhear the interpretation of a dream of one of the enemy soldiers. From this he learned of the panic felt by the Midianites. Now, armed with new confidence, a new strategy, and in the might of the Lord, Gideon led his three hundred faithful warriors to victory over what before had seemed to be insurmountable odds.

We Have a Tough God

This story of how the Lord confronted the problems facing Israel underlines a most important point. We have a tough, problem-confronting, problem-solving God. He does not retreat from either the problems we have brought on ourselves or the problems life has dished out. And He wants to make us much tougher people. He wants to give us a new perspective on our problems, exercise our prayer muscles, and strengthen the fiber of our souls. Instead of wringing our hands in consternation or running away in panic, He wants to make us people He can use.

Just as the Lord changed Gideon's attitude and then strengthened and used him in the midst of his problems, so He wants to transform our approach to problems. He wants us to think of ourselves as being men and women of valor because of His might at work in us. And He assures us that His abiding presence is available to help us tackle every problem with His strength and direction—confident that problems are not a sign of His absence.

This, then, is our assurance—when a problem distresses us, we can be sure that the Lord wants to enlist us as a person who will trust Him completely. Our challenge is to seek His will for a solution to the problem, and move forward with boldness and courage.

We all have problems. That's life. But we also have a Lord who not only helps us grow through our problems, but gives us the power to triumph over them.

2

WHEN PROBLEMS
PILE UP

RECENTLY, A LADY WROTE, "Lloyd, there is just one word to describe my state of mind when problems begin to pile up—panic! I can handle them fairly well with the Lord's help when they come at me one at a time, but when they begin to stack up one on top of the other, I begin to fall apart."

We've all felt that way at times. Often, like this lady, our response is panic. It is the panic of wondering if we can make it through when a multiplicity of trials descend on us all at once.

It's one thing to say that God allows a problem to surface because He wants to accomplish His plans and purposes in us, our relationships, or our society. But it's something else to continue to trust Him when these problems pile up. Life becomes a sea of problems with waves and breakers hitting us on every side.

We can take one problem if we can concentrate all our energies on solving it. But so often those energies are distracted by other problems which explode at the same time.

For example, we face a problem at work. We press on with

courage, seeking a solution. Then another problem hits us at home, and another with a friend. We try to stay afloat when another wave of problems almost engulfs us at church or in the community. Then, as if we didn't have enough of our own problems, we are pulled by the undertow of the problems of people we love. We'd like to be able to say, "Well, that's their problem!" but we still feel the impact of their difficulties. It's then that panic sets in and we wonder how much we can take. Most of all, we long for the storm on the turbulent waters of life to return to some semblance of calm again.

Problems have a way of building up. They accumulate, and suddenly, too many surface at the same time. Sometimes it's our own fault. We've neglected lots of potential problems saying, "I'll worry about that tomorrow." Or we put off caring about the people of our lives, and then they all want our attention and help at the same time.

As one man expressed it, "I wish the people at the office, my wife, my kids, and my friends could have a conference and decide to schedule their individual crises one at a time on a reasonable agenda and in a way I could handle. Why can't the people in my life see when I'm under the pressure of a pile of problems and hold off until I catch my breath?"

That's asking a lot. Here's how his wife reacts to his complaint. "When's a good time to share my problems? My husband is under pressure most of the time. If I waited to talk to him about them, he'd never be ready. Sometimes I store up my problems hoping to catch him at a time when he can really listen to what's happening to me and the family. Sometimes I've made the foolish mistake of bringing them up on a quiet evening together or when we're on vacation. That usually ruins our time together. I have to admit, though, when I see he has time for other problems, there's an urge to be sure he cares about mine also. I get that 'What about me? What about the kids' needs? What about our problems?' kind of feeling."

We can empathize with both this husband and his wife.

It would be so much simpler if life would present us with problems in a more orderly and timely way so we could handle them one at a time. We wonder if our panic actually increases the desire of others to pile their problems on us when we've got more than enough of our own. We tend to become almost paranoid as we wonder what problem will hit next.

A Promise from the Lord

Is there a promise from the Lord for those times when problems pile up? Can He do anything to help us in the midst of the raging storms of multiplied difficulties? Yes, of course He can! His promise for times like that is found in Isaiah 43:1–2. "Fear not, for I have redeemed you; I have called *you* by name; you are Mine. When you pass through the waters I *will be* with you; and through the rivers, they shall not overflow you" (italics mine).

This promise was given to Israel during the exile in Babylon. The Jews felt forgotten by their God as the problems of being in a strange and foreign land mounted. They were lonesome for Palestine, for a renewed closeness with the Lord, and for an assurance that He knew and cared about them. Fear, anxiety, and discouragement mounted in equal proportion with their multiplied problems. And this word from the Lord was exactly what they needed.

At the same time, it is a word that we need today when problems build up. In these verses we find two essential assurances for us to claim when the storms of life hit with hurricane force on the turbulent sea of our problems.

We are told not to fear. The Hebrew verb translated "fear not" has the sense of meaning "do not gaze about in anxiety." When our problems pile up we are tempted to focus on circumstances and people. We have a feeling of "Why me?" But the secret of riding out the storms is in keeping our attention on the Lord. We can't do that for long, though, unless we know that we are the focus of His attention. So the "fear not" of His promise is inseparable from his affirmation "I have redeemed you; I have called you by your name; you are Mine." The key to understanding this is in the Hebrew word for "redeemed," which means "to purchase back, reclaim, repossess."

These words are brimming over with liberating, fear-dispelling hope. No matter what happens to us, our sure anchor is the faithfulness of the Lord. He knows each of us by name. He cares about us, and nothing can happen that will make Him stop loving us. We belong to the Lord.

For us, the "fear not, I have redeemed you" assurance is reclaimed at the cross of Christ. He purchased our salvation at the high cost of His own blood. He bought us back, and in spite of all we've said or done or the lack of courage we may have displayed in our problems, we belong to Him forever. And our new name? Forgiven, liberated, empowered, cherished, and beloved. We are of infinite value to Him. He will not forget us when we need Him. After all He's done to redeem us, He will not leave or forsake us to drift in panic in life's storms.

When problems pile up, we have a song for the long night of difficulty. The lyrics for that triumphant song were written by the Apostle Paul who had learned how to trust the Lord in the howling winds of adversity. "And we know that all things work together for good to those who love God, to those who are the called according to His purpose. For whom He foreknew, He also predestined to be conformed to the image of His Son, that He might be the firstborn among many brethren. Moreover whom He predestined, these He also called; whom He called, these He also justified; and whom He justified, these He also glorified. What shall we say to these things? If God is for us, who can be against us?" (Rom. 8:28–31). That is our song when problems pile up. But we're not supposed to stop there. Dare to ask Paul's question, "Who shall separate us from the love of Christ? Shall tribulation, or distress, or persecution, or famine, or nakedness, or peril, or sword? . . ." Then our song, sung above the crashing waves, will be: "Yet in all these things we are more than conquerors through Him who loved us" (Rom. 8:35, 37).

The second part of God's promise to Israel in the captivity was the assurance that they would make it through their distressing time. "When you pass through the waters, I *will be* with you; and through the rivers, they shall not overflow you" (Isa. 43:2, italics mine). With these words the Lord reminded His people of two pivotal historical events—the Red Sea crossing into the wilderness and the crossing of the River Jordan into the promised land of Canaan. In both events the Lord had intervened to protect and open the way of progress for His people to move forward. "Waters" had become a metaphor for troubles and "rivers" was a metaphor for the formidable obstacles standing against people and their goals.

The important word in this part of the Lord's promise is "through." He would get His people *through* the difficulties they faced. When we know and understand that great truth, we can handle any problem that comes our way. If we know that victory is assured we can face any battle. And how can we have courage in the midst of the battle? Only by raw faith in Him who is with us who says, "When you pass through the waters, I will be with you." No wind is too strong, no wave too high, no crashing breaker too irresistible, no undertow too formidable.

Ten Things to Do When Problems Pile Up

But how do we claim this awesome promise? How does it work for us in the midst of our storms? These are questions I've confronted in my own life. And as I've wrestled with them, the Lord has given me ten steps, all based on the promise of Isaiah 43:1–2. Each one gives me a way to reach out and grasp the help the Lord offers. I share them with you because they have helped me come through the waters of problems instead of being overcome by them.

1. Focus on the Lord, not circumstances. The first thing to do when we are confronted with difficult problems is to focus on the Lord and not the problems. So often, our immediate reaction to a problem is alarm and fear. "What am I going to do?" we say, before we have asked for the Lord's presence and power in the problem. When problems strike, we need the Lord. And when we seek Him and not an immediate solution, we give Him a chance to provide us with the strength and courage we need. I believe God uses our problems to call us into a deeper relationship with Him. We can pray, "Lord, for some reason in Your infinite wisdom, You have allowed these problems to surface because You are ready to work in and through me to do Your will. I claim Your promise to be with me all the way through to solutions that are best for me and all concerned. I deliberately turn my eyes to You and away from the problems. I trust You completely to deal with these problems in Your perfect timing and way."

That quality of prayer releases us from the tension of trying to solve problems in our own strength. It affirms that our relationship with the Lord is more crucial to us than making Him our "fix-it" God. We claim that He knows, cares, and is with us through it all.

2. Face the problem. In the strength of a renewed relationship of love with the Lord we are now ready for the second step—to face the problems as they are. Our renewed companionship with the Lord enables us to do that with ruthless honesty. So many problems engulf us with fear before we take a good look at them, unwrapping them and examining all the aspects of them. Then we can ask the Lord to show us the potential for good wrapped inside of each problem. "Lord, what do You want me to learn, discover, do, or be through this problem?"

As we wait for the answer to that prayer, we can rest in complete confidence that the Lord will show us the good that can come from our difficult and hard times. Remember that the Lord allows problems to surface because He wants to accomplish something in us, in our loved ones and friends, and in the world around us. Our task is to ask what His purpose is and then to cooperate in the full realization of it.

3. Thank the Lord. Next, remember that in thanking the Lord for the problems we are also affirming His presence. Thanksgiving affirms that He knows and cares and will use the problem for our growth and the fulfillment of His purposes. Thanksgiving brings release, the easing of tension, and the freedom of trust. Praising the Lord in a problem is our ultimate level of surrender. It opens us up to the flow of the Lord's Spirit in us and in the problems. It isn't that the problems are good in and of themselves, but that they are the occasion for deeper trust and for progress.

Recently, a friend said to me, "How can I thank God for this problem? It's difficult, painful, and distressing." My response was, "Naturally, you aren't going to feel that the problem of itself is particularly beneficial. But you can be thankful that the Lord will use it to work out needed changes in your own life. Furthermore, He will enable you to overcome the problem for His glory." When my friend took this attitude he got free of the resentment and fear that were blocking him from receiving the help the Lord was trying to give him. And in working through toward the solution he was given wisdom beyond his understanding about how to handle the problem and finally overcame it. In the process, he grew immensely as a person and became the Lord's agent of reconciliation in what had seemed to be an insolvable problem.

Another friend of mine accepted the challenge to experiment with a thirty-day discipline of thanksgiving. The experiment broke the bonds of negative thinking. During that time, she concentrated on the positive potential of her problems. From the moment of waking up in the morning until she dropped off to sleep at night, she centered her thinking on being thankful for whatever happened.

When a difficulty painted her into a corner of frustration, she thanked the Lord, knowing that He would show her the way out. As the days passed, she felt a new closeness with the Lord, a oneness as a problem-solving partner with Him. Life became one endless prayer of thanksgiving. This is what she says: "What began as a thirty-day experiment now has become the strategy of my life for facing and solving problems. When I thank the Lord for problems as they arise, I really am released from tension and become open to supernatural strength and insight I would never have been able to generate on my own. Problems upset me only when I take my eyes off the Lord and forget to thank Him for counting me worthy to be a person He can use to tackle and work through problems and one who can trust Him for the answers. If I had never had problems, think of what I would have missed!"

4. Put blame behind you. The fourth step is not easy for most of us. It is to put blame behind us. When a problem hits, it really doesn't make much difference who caused it. If the blame is ours, we need to confess that and accept forgiveness. When other people are the culprits, we will have no peace or strength to confront the problem until we forgive them.

Seeking to blame—ourselves or others—exhausts the energy we need to use in solving the problem. Often we muddle about trying to identify the one who caused the problem. Understanding the cause may help us to avoid further recurrences of the problem, but blame usually stands in the way of receiving the Lord's power for a solution. The Lord is interested in resolutions, not recriminations. Instead of wallowing in self-pity, we need to get on with what needs to be learned and done according to His will. Rather than waiting, immobilized in long periods of blame, we need to get on with the business of living.

I know a man who has a miserable marriage simply because he insists on laying a heavy load of blame on his wife for every difficulty that rocks their home. He focuses on her short-comings and is always ready to point out that these are the cause of most of their problems. He's not alone in this, though. Think of those times we've made little attempt to get on with a solution to a problem because we wanted to expose people involved or wanted them to stew in the juices of our "I told you so" blame.

When problems invade your life, don't blame yourself, don't blame other people, don't even blame God. Get at the problem. Confess your failures and forgive them in others. But at all costs, put blame behind you!

5. Pray for guidance. The fifth step is reflective prayer. Any problem worthy of our concern deserves concentrated thought guided by the Lord. Setting aside a time at the beginning of each day for a review of the problems facing us gives the Lord access to our thinking brain. This exercise involves more than running down through our list of problems. After we have talked to the Lord about our problems, thanking Him for them and what He will do, we need to sit quietly and wait for Him to give us thoughts, insights, and the action steps we are to take in solving the problem. He is able to get through to us. He enables us to see things differently from His perspective.

Often big problems demand an even longer period of quiet. At such times, it is helpful to set aside a day, or an afternoon to get away by ourselves to think and reflect prayerfully. These mini-retreats can transform our perception and attitudes. Also, some people do their prayer-thinking while taking a long walk. Whatever method we use, we can know that the Lord is ready to help us if we will give Him a chance.

I have a friend who schedules a half-hour each morning, a three-hour period each week, and a full day each month just to spread out before the Lord the problems he's facing and to receive His guidance. Those of us who are close to him are constantly amazed at his resiliency and the seemingly limitless energy he brings to problem solving. We should not be surprised; he is living in the flow of the Lord's wisdom.

6. *Share the problems.* There are times when the Lord also uses other people in assisting us with our problems. So the next step is to share our problems with a small group of trusted friends. These should be people on whom we can depend for prayer and encouragement. God, our Father, delights when His children bear each other's burdens. In fact, friends are resources of His strength and guidance whom He deploys when we affirm our mutual dependence and share our needs. Often the Lord will use a friend to give us insights that have escaped us or which we may have resisted. We were never meant to face life's problems alone.

I've found it important to have a few trusted friends who are also open to share their needs with me. This frees me to be honest with them about my problems. These should be people who are genuinely interested in us and will listen intently without interrupting with precipitous advice. When I meet with the people in my own support group, I know they care for me. None of us has a personal axe to grind or attempts to manipulate another person as we share and talk out our concerns. I would not want to face the problems of life without the people-power of these friends. And the Lord never meant that I should try.

7. *Become your own best friend.* Next, dare to be your own best friend. Problems have a way of getting us down on ourselves. We entertain the lingering thought that if we were better, stronger people, problems wouldn't attack us. Ridiculous! That denies the truth that great people are those who can confront and grapple with truly difficult problems.

The best way to define what it would mean for us to be our own best friend is to think about the kind of friend we need when we have problems. Remember the people who have been a help in times of problems—the kind of people who don't minimize the problem, but communicate their trust and confidence in us to confront, solve, and overcome the problems. These are people who believe in us, who know that given the chance, we will do the right thing with courage and daring.

Good friends help us analyze the problem, take it apart, and examine it for what it really is. They are sensitive in acknowledging our confession of anything we have done to cause or contribute to the problem. But, they are also quick to alert us to any evidence of self-condemnation or false guilt. A true friend will blow a whistle on prolonged remorse or blaming of people. Most of all, a good friend knows how to listen until we have explained our view of the problem. Then he goes on to ask, "Well, what can you learn from this, how can you grow through it, and what are the steps to be taken in a creative solution?"

Is it possible to be that kind of person to ourselves? Yes! In times of problems we urgently need to affirm ourselves as loved by the Lord and capable of receiving the supernatural strength He offers to work through whatever faces us. We are to forgive ourselves for any part we have played in producing the problem without heaping any kind of emotional garbage on ourselves for past failures. Then we need to develop our self-image as problem-solvers by the Lord's strength and for His glory. Being as gracious to ourselves as God is frees us either to do what needs to be done or to wait patiently for the Lord's timing and guidance. This is what Paul meant when he said, "I can do all things through Christ who strengthens me."

8. *Claim a specific promise.* Next, as we remember that there is a perfectly matched promise from the Lord for every problem that can ever strike us, we claim that specific promise for the problem confronting us.

To say that the Lord has a perfectly matched promise for our every problem is a bold statement. How do we know it is a fact? I believe we can be sure of it as by faith we see that all of God's promises since the beginning of time are fulfilled in Jesus Christ—Immanuel, God with us! Paul gives substance to that truth when he writes, "For all the promises of God in Him are Yes, and in Him Amen, to the glory of God through us" (2 Cor. 1:20). All of the promises of power, intervention, forgiveness, wisdom, guidance, and overcoming courage are available to us as we face our problems. Through Christ, God has confronted evil, sin, suffering, death, and fear, and through the cross and the resurrection, He has won. And now the glorified Christ is the all-powerful presence of God with us. His awesome promise is that He will dwell in us. We are never alone.

It is the victorious Christ in us who confronts our problems with us and for us. He is the healing power of God for our physical and emotional ills, the forgiving power of our problems with guilt, the reconciler of our broken relationships, the source of light in the darkness of indecision, the peace we need in times of jittery nerves, the courage to go on against seemingly insurmountable odds, the assurance that nothing can ultimately defeat us. When problems strike, He will reiterate one of the promises perfectly suited for our condition. And our response? To say with Paul, "Yes . . . Amen. So be it!"

9. Take the first step. Fortified with the particular promise of the Lord suited for each problem, we can accept His gift of courage and take the first step in solving the problem. We are meant to be gifted people, those who untangle problems with a special endowment from the Lord. In each problem we are given supernatural power in one of the many spiritual gifts offered us. He gives us wisdom to know His mind and plan, discernment to see all the issues, faith to claim and expect His intervention, power to pray for His healing in us and between us and others, and confidence to boldly anticipate His miracles.

And He offers something more—His own character—in the fruit of His own indwelling Spirit: love, joy, peace, patience, kindness, goodness, faithfulness, gentleness, and self-control (Gal. 5:22–23). When we confess to the Lord that we cannot solve the problem on our own, He invades our minds with qualities and capabilities beyond our limited abilities. After we are through the turmoil of a big problem and look back, we are amazed not only by what the Lord did to change the people and circumstances involved in the problem, but also by what He did to graciously prepare and equip us.

The Lord frees us to take the first step. We can ask, "Lord, what can I do or say today that will move me forward to the accomplishment of Your resolution of this problem?" Obedience is the key of spiritual knowledge and the further release of power for subsequent steps. The Lord gives us the goal and vision of the solution according to His plan. Then He gives us courage to get moving under His direction.

10. Prepare for the next problem. The last step in dealing with problems is to glorify the Lord for what He has done in and through us and then get set for what is out ahead. Our present difficulties are preparation for trusting the Lord in future problems. And even as we can be certain that new problems will come, we can be just as sure that God's grace and power will always be with us.

The Lord is continuing His creation and calls us to be co-creators with Him in our own transformation, growth, and development as whole persons. He has called us to live at our maximum capability. And all the problems in us, between us as persons, and in our society will be but opportunities to discover the Lord's sufficiency for whatever happens.

I know that is true. I have been a Christian for thirty-five years. All through those years, the Lord has helped me face and conquer problems. In each difficulty, I have learned more of Him and His ways. He's never let me down. And all that I've discovered thus far is constantly drawn on in confronting present problems. We often talk about the "school of hard knocks." I'd rather call it the "school of gentle molding." The Lord graciously brings us through each problem and shapes our character to be more like His own.

I cannot remember a time in my Christian experience when I was totally free of problems. Good thing! Right now I'm facing one of those times of problems piling up, but I feel no panic. As I consider each one of the problems in the pile, I know from previous experience with similar problems how the Lord will deal with it. Most of all, I know He is with me. And I know that what I'm learning from Him presently will become part of the reservoir of training which will be used in the future.

In his book *The Changed Life*, Henry Drummond said, "The eternal life, the life of faith, is simply a life of higher vision. Faith is an attitude—a mirror set at right angle. To become like Christ is the only thing in the world worth caring for, the thing before which every ambition of man is folly, and all lower achievement vain." With the mirror set at right angle, I see more than life's problems, I see the Lord at work in them, and through them, in me.

Added to our personal growth through problems is our preparation to be a sensitive, empathetical friend to others who are facing their own problems. The precious words, "I understand" can only be spoken by us when we have lived in depth. And our understanding will come from having been through what others are facing. So often when I listen to people share their problems, my mind flashes back to a similar problem I have been through. What I learned from the Lord in it becomes the basis of insight and tender concern. Whenever I can draw on what I've discovered from the Lord in my problem to help others, I know that it's all been worth it.

We're going to spell out all this in the chapters that follow. As we do that, stand firm on this basic conviction: problems are an evidence that God cares and will use us as His agents in solving them.

The waves of the sea of life's problems will not drown us. Present with us and in us, the Lord says, "When you pass through the waters, I will be with you" (Isa. 43:2). Annie Johnson Flint put this magnificently in a poem I cherish. It reminds me that it is because God cares that I still have problems and that He will guide me *through* them.

Passing Through

"When Thou passest through the waters,"
  Deep the waves may be, and cold,
But Jehovah is our refuge
  And His promise is our hold;
For the Lord Himself hath said it,
  He the faithful God and true;
When thou comest to the waters,
  Thou shalt *not go down,* but *through.*

Seas of sorrow, seas of trial,
  Bitterest anguish, fiercest pain,
Rolling surges of temptation,
  Sweeping over heart and brain,
They shall never overflow us,
  For we know His word is true;
All His waves and all His billows
  He will *lead us safely through.*

Threatening breakers of destruction,
  Doubt's insidious undertow,
Shall not sink us, shall not drag us
  Out to ocean depths of woe;
For His promise shall sustain us,
  Praise the Lord, whose word is true!
We shall not go down or under,
  He hath said, "Thou passest *through.*"

3

LET UP,
EASE OFF,
LET GO!

RIGHT FROM THE BEGINNING it had been one of those stress-filled days. My alarm clock didn't go off on time. When I awoke with a start an hour later than I planned, my pulsebeat quickened with the panic that I had missed an important breakfast meeting. Quickly checking my watch I realized that if I made a mad dash to the shower and got dressed at break-neck speed I just might make the meeting on time.

In the rush I had to forgo my usual quiet time of prayer and meditation. I knew that was perilous with the jam-packed schedule I had ahead of me that day. So I prayed as I got ready and drove to my breakfast appointment, but the quick prayers did little to calm my mind or my pulse.

The meeting was demanding and required concentration. The problem that was the focus of the breakfast conversation didn't get settled, nor did the bacon and eggs I ate. As soon as we adjourned, I rushed off to several other meetings that had been scheduled back-to-back all through the morning, noon, and into the afternoon.

By late afternoon, I was exhausted. Travel between meetings had been filled with congested traffic, blaring horns, and screeching tires. In the offices I visited, telephones rang incessantly and people talked in agitated, pressured tones. Noise and distraction dogged my steps all day.

As I ended the busy round of meetings and appointments and drove back to my office, I reflected on the day. It was then I realized that I had neglected two important things because of oversleeping. I had not had my quiet time with the Lord to pray about the day's problems, and I had not taken my vitamins.

Now, I'm no health nut, but I do find that taking vitamins helps me handle the pressures of a physically draining schedule.

As I drove along, I remembered that my supply of vitamins was running low and decided to stop at a health food store to pick up some more. While I was browsing around the shelves of the store, my attention was arrested by a sign advertising a new vitamin formula.

"Add zip and zest to your life!" the sign promised. Below that was the name of the product. And then at the bottom of the sign was a "got-to-have-it" sales motivator. It read, "Now at last—A Vitamin Formula for Busy People Who Need to Stay Calm in a Noisy, Stress-filled World."

"How did they know about me?" I wondered as I picked up a box of vitamins and read the promises about what the product would do for people who need added energy and fortification for the demands of life.

You guessed it—I bought some! When I returned to my office and began to open the package I discovered a small, credit-card-sized plastic card. Upon closer examination I read that it was a biofeedback device for monitoring your stress level. Overlaid on the card was a black square of sensitized material that was supposed to register the amount of stress in your body when you pressed your thumb on the square for a count of ten.

The instructions on the card described the stress test: "If the black square remains black you are stressed; if it turns red you are tense; if it goes green you are normal; if it becomes blue you are calm."

I couldn't resist the temptation to find out how I was doing at the moment. I pressed my thumb on the square and held it there longer than the count of ten just to give myself every advantage. Much to my consternation the color didn't change—it remained a convicting black. Assuming that I had not held my thumb on the card long enough, I repeated the experiment. Still black!

I don't know whether that little card was capable of accurately monitoring my physical and emotional condition, but I do know that it helped impress on me the realization that once again I had taken over the management of my life and had fallen victim of the noisy, blaring world of stress. The Lord has clever ways of getting through to us, doesn't He?—even to using a sign in a health food store and a handy biofeedback card!

But here is the rest of the story. As I examined that little biofeedback card again, I saw that it also contained instructions on how to relax. The "let go" approach was urged in all four of the steps to relaxation. First, I was told to take a deep breath and hold it. After counting to ten, I was to release the breath and let my body go limp. Next, I was instructed to make fists of both hands, and at the count of ten I was to relax them and let my body go limp. Third, while breathing normally, I was to count back from ten to zero and exhale with each number. Fourth, I was told to imagine myself lying in the warm sun on the beach or soaking in a hot tub. And as I lay there I was to imagine myself getting warm all over.

When I finished those four exercises, I was so relaxed physically that I wanted to abandon my plan to study late into the evening and go home and hop into bed. But I also realized that even though my body was relaxed, my mind and spirit were not. I needed something more for that than relaxation techniques. Letting go of the body's tensions does not assure peace of mind or soul.

Wouldn't it be great if we had a spiritual feedback card to test our level of trust and confident relaxation in our relationship with God? And yet, we do have a built-in alarm system. When our bodies are tense and our emotions feel distressed, it is a sure sign that something is wrong at a deeper level in our souls.

The Big Problem of Inner Tension

When I asked people all across America to share with me their feelings about problems, I learned for sure that even though they believed in God they were troubled by life's tensions and pressures. Why is this? So many of them expressed frustration over the fact that they were so preoccupied with trying to handle their internal problems that they were unable to creatively cope with their external problems.

We can quickly identify with that dilemma! We all live in two worlds—the inner world of our own private thoughts and feelings and the outer world of our relationships and responsibilities in our families, among our friends, at work, in our churches, and in our communities. Both worlds dramatically affect each other.

The problems we face in the world around us do have an impact on our inner world. We ruminate and brood over them when they happen and long afterward. Memories of previous problems, many still unresolved, limit our ability to grapple with present difficulties. Tension builds, robbing us of an inner sense of calm and well being. Over the years, we become increasingly insecure. Then, as the world around us dishes out new problems, we project our inner turmoil onto them and actually multiply the problems. Or what's even worse, we create problems in our outer world because of the turbulent unrest inside us.

Our tendency is to blame what's happening around us for

the distress within us. Usually, just the opposite is true. How we react to life's challenges is a tell-tale exposure of what's going on inside in our inner selves.

When the Frantic Becomes the Familiar

Many of us find being frantic more familiar than the pleasure of being calm. We actually look for distress because it is more familiar to us than being confidently quiet. Even among believing, committed Christians, the old patterns of agitated nerves, overpressured schedules, conflicts with people, and disturbing stress have become so much the expected that we are in danger of making difficulties bigger than they are.

We hear a great deal these days about the problem of noise pollution. We live in a noisy society that keeps us in constant agitation. Added to the clashing, clanging noise of our congested, urbanized, jet-travel society, we are bombarded by the endless sounds of television, radio, and the omnipresent blaring of music systems in most every store or office in which we find ourselves. And then there is the distressing impact of ringing telephones, the whir of all our machines and appliances in our highly mechanized living.

But that's not all. We are a part of a culture that talks until it knows what it wants to say. We abhor quiet like nature abhors a vacuum. Talk, talk, talk! We talk it over, talk it up, and talk it through. And yet, with all our talking we still fail to understand each other.

And finally, we are polluted by the "noise" of so much of what we read. It is the bad news—the jangling news that makes block letter headlines. We are bombarded by the bold print that describes terrorist action, threat of nuclear war, murder, kidnapping, and suffering.

All this keeps us on edge and distraught. How can we take it? The point is—we can't! It is impossible to handle it unless we possess an inner calm and quietness. Without that, our external world of clamor and noise becomes unbearable. And

what's even more serious, we will be incapable of doing anything creative to help change the problems in the world around
us.

A Promise for Inner Noise Tension

Once again, the problem is perfectly matched by a promise
from the Lord. His promise for the problem of inner tension
is, "Be still, and know that I am God; I will be exalted among
the nations, I will be exalted in the earth! The Lord of hosts
is with us; the God of Jacob is our refuge" (Ps. 46:10–11).

It is helpful to consider the background of the context of
this magnificent promise. Psalm 46 recounts the Lord's intervention to save Jerusalem at the time of the Assyrians' siege
when Hezekiah was king. Sennacherib surrounded the city
with one hundred and eighty thousand soldiers. There seemed
to be no hope. And then, at five minutes to twelve, just before
the attack, a plague struck the Assyrian army and most of
them died. The Lord had saved the city.

When we read the Psalm 46 again with this background
in mind, the psalmist's words take on new meaning for us.
When problems threaten to overwhelm us, we can say, "God
is our refuge and strength, a very present help in trouble.
Therefore we will not fear . . ." (v. 1). Then we can trust
our future to Him. When we are besieged and surrounded
by seemingly impossible odds, we can say of our lives what
the psalmist said of Jerusalem: "God is in the midst of her,
she shall not be moved; God shall help her, just at the break
of dawn" (v. 5). God promises that if we are still, we shall
know that He is God over our circumstances. He will be exalted in our problems.

Here is an admonition with an assurance, a promise of peace
in a distressing world filled with the tension of noisy problems.
These two verses of Psalm 46 are really a dialogue. First God
speaks and then the psalmist responds. The Lord tells us what
to do to realize a momentous promise, and the psalmist responds with a liberating conviction about how we can live

out that promise. Considered carefully, these verses show us a three-step progression of experiencing profound, quiet confidence in our souls which can be expressed in all of our problems.

Let Up, Ease Off, and Let Go

The first step to this true, lasting calm is to "be still." The Lord wants us to discover inner stillness that can be sustained in the fast moving pace of our busy lives. I have often pondered what being "still" really means. I have falsely associated it with uninterrupted times of absolute silence alone with the Lord, away from the world's impertinent noise. And yet, so often when I carve out of my schedule a few days for quiet study and prayer, I discover that the absence of the noise of our culture does not assure stillness or quiet.

This is because of the noise inside me. I still hear the noises of demanding people and the sounds of unresolved problems. But there is a deeper source of discordant noise pollution. It comes from my urgent voice of self-will arguing with the Lord over what's best for me and for the people of my life, or the problems I face. Stillness eludes me. I can't hear what the Lord wants to say in the inner voice of thought and inspiration.

One day I discovered the deeper meaning of the Hebrew word found in the forty-sixth psalm for "be still." It changed my understanding of what the Lord requires before His promises of calm stillness can be realized inside us or around us. It really means "leave off." The implication is, "let up, let go, ease off." Stillness is surrender. It's being willing to do nothing until we are able to allow God to do what only He can do and He has given us clear direction of what He wants us to do.

Letting go isn't easy. We think we know what's best for us. And we forge ahead before we have clear guidance from the Lord. We want the Lord's help, but are reluctant to give Him complete control. That sets up more discordant noise than any amount of the turned up decibels of our noisy world. It's the blaring pollution of petulant willfulness. We get pushy with the Almighty!

Unfortunately, though, we usually have to make a mess of things before we either cry out for God's help or trust Him completely. Sometimes we can endure excruciating problems for months, even years, before we finally give up trying to solve them ourselves. It's amazing how long and hard we hang on to our predetermined ideas of what is needed to resolve the difficulties.

When the late Dr. Henrietta Mears, the great Christian educator, was asked what she would do differently if she had her life to live over, she said, "I'd trust God more." If that question was asked of me, I'd say the same thing except I would add " . . . and sooner." We often wait until problems are multiplied by our own efforts to solve them with our own insight and strength before we finally surrender them to the Lord. That pride and willfulness keep us from being creative cooperators with the Lord in solving problems by His strength and strategy.

Let Go and Know God

We are promised that when we are still, when we stop trying to solve our problems on our own, we shall then *know* God. The noise of the static of our souls will be silenced enough not only to receive His guidance but to receive Him!

The Hebrew verb "to know" implies much more than the accumulation of ideas or even convictions about God. It means intimate communion and companionship, a Thou-I relationship, a Person-to-person oneness. For Christians that begins with His gracious approach to us in Christ. He is always the initiator and instigator of a relationship with Himself. He communicates His unqualified love, creates in us a desire to know Him, and then liberates us with the gift of faith to trust Him.

The only way we can truly know God is in His own presence

with us in Jesus Christ. Christ is Immanuel—God with us. The more we know of Christ, the more we know of God. Jesus made this very clear when He said, "I am the way, the truth, and the life. No one comes to the Father except through Me. If you had *known* Me, you would have *known* My Father also; from now on you *know* Him and have seen Him" (John 14:6–7, italics mine). These words were spoken to the disciples on the night before Jesus was crucified. They mean so much more to us from this side of Calvary, an open tomb, and Pentecost. In Christ's life and message we know what God is like. But in His death we experience His acceptance and forgiving love. Now nothing can stand in the way of knowing Him.

In the resurrection the enemy of death was defeated and life in abundance now and eternal life throughout all eternity are ours. That's sealed in the Master's own will and testament, "This is eternal life, that they may know You, the only true God, and Jesus Christ whom You have sent" (John 17:3). Christ is our Mediator in the joyous experience of knowing God. Paul declared this good news: "For there is one God and one Mediator between God and men, the Man Christ Jesus . . ." (1 Tim. 2:5). And the post-resurrection, post-Pentecost dwelling of the Mediator is in our minds and hearts. The mystery of how to know God in depth is now an open secret: ". . . the mystery which has been hidden from ages and from generations, but now has been revealed to His saints. To them God willed to make known what are the riches of the glory of this mystery among the Gentiles: which is Christ in you, the hope of glory" (Col. 1:26–27).

Now we can understand what it means to "be still and know." Stillness—letting up, easing off, letting go—is the result of knowing God in His indwelling presence in Christ in that inner world of our private self we talked about earlier. Reigning within us, Christ heals the memories of failures in previous problems that make us so unsure of ourselves in present problems. He places His forgiving cross between us and our incrimination of ourselves and declares an armistice in the civil war inside us. He imparts new self-esteem to us rooted in His gift of courage and daring. Our inner world is filled with His peace and we can face the outer world of conflict and difficulties. At last, we are Christ-inspired problem-solvers who, with His help, are able to do something about the things that previously threw us into a tailspin.

It's amazing, though, how few Christians today have claimed the power of the indwelling Lord. They believe in Him as Savior but side-step His lordship over their inner hearts. W. E. Sangster put it pointedly. "It is not enough—let it be said reverently—it is not enough to have Christ near to us. Oh, it is wonderful, of course, in contrast with not even believing in His existence at all or knowing Him only as a name, but, for the highest spiritual life, it is not enough. You see, we do most of our living inside us. Our thinking, feeling, and willing are all within. External events press upon us, but they have meaning only by our inward interpretation. We discover that when we are dealing with the troubles of life. The important thing is not what happens to us but what happens in us. The same thing can happen to two different people and a precisely different thing happens in them. . . . If, therefore, we are to be helped in our battle against temptation and in our war with fear and worry, selfishness, and greed, we must have help within. Not there, but here! Not outside, but inside."*

A man who is missing this "inside story" came to see me one afternoon a couple of weeks ago. After some opening pleasantries, I asked him what I could pray for in his life. His quick, glib response was, "I want to know the Lord better!"

I suspected he didn't really understand what he was asking. So I pressed him a bit. "How do you think that could happen?" His response was very significant, "Oh, I'd begin to take time for prayer, start reading the Bible more consistently, and try harder to serve the Lord."

---

* W. E. Sangster, *Can I Know God?* (Nashville: Abingdon Press), p. 171.

Do you notice anything lacking in that response? I did, because I've been where that man was. Everything he said was an expression of self-effort. Of course, the Lord wants to reveal more of His nature through our prayer, our Bible reading, and our concern to serve Him. But the missing ingredient in my friend's reply was the very thing the Lord wants most. He wants to get to the depth of us, and He can do that only as we yield ourselves and our problems to Him.

Many of us, like my friend, pray, study, and seek to serve but still do not really know God simply because we have missed the progression and interaction of *being* and *doing.* We attempt to do what we want to do for the Lord, or what we think He wants us to do, before experiencing a knowing relationship with Him rooted in consistent, faithful surrender. Submission is the key to knowing Him, and knowing Him as indwelling Lord is the source of the guidance for what we are to do. William Law stated it succinctly, "A Christ not in us . . . is a Christ not ours."

In the light of all we've considered about the problem-solving power of the indwelling Lord, we can appreciate more fully His promise to be still and know Him. And the more we know Him, the more still we become. Now we can experience the third aspect of the promise He gives in Psalm 46. He will be exalted in all things. "I will be exalted among the nations, I will be exalted in the earth" (v. 10).

God Exalted in Our Problems

There is an irrevocableness about the sound of that promise. It is as if the Lord gives an assurance and a warning. In the focus of our discussion of problems, it is as if He says, "I will be exalted in your problems. Be sure of that! There will be no other way." The word "exalted" in this verse refers to both what will happen to us and to our relationship with the Lord. Exalted means elevated, raised up, praised. It also carries the meaning of being intensely joyous.

We see then that God will be glorified through our problems

and we will feel an unfettered, joyous praise for what He will do. Put another way, the way the Lord helps us in our problems will make us love Him all the more and will lead us to trust even more completely. He's exalted when we surrender our problems and patiently trust Him, praising Him for what He will do in us and then through us.

The Lord's word to Israel through the psalmist is that how He cares for His people will cause Him to be exalted among all the nations of the earth. That has very personal implications for you and me. When problems come and we are still, we become the focus of His providential care. The way He helps us will astonish our friends and even our enemies. He will give us strength that will produce an observable strength and courage about us that will prompt others to want to know Him.

Our Response and Confidence for the Future

Psalm 46 concludes with the psalmist's response to the magnificent promise God has given. I sense he has moved through the progressive steps of releasing his needs to the Lord and has been introduced to a new and personal relationship with Him. Knowing how the Lord had been exalted because of His intervention during the siege of Jerusalem, the psalmist now had confidence for the future. "The Lord of hosts is with us; the God of Jacob is our refuge" (v. 11). The familiar biblical phrase "the Lord of hosts" means the all-encompassing dominion of God over the whole universe. All the host of heaven, angelic messengers, and all the forces of nature are at His command and can be deployed for our help in time of need.

The term "God of Jacob" personalizes this even further. The God who used all that Jacob went through until he trusted the Lord completely and became Israel, is the Lord on whom we depend. He took a jealous, conniving, manipulative, ambitious person and turned him into a great man. Over and over throughout Jacob's life the Lord allowed problems to surface in which Jacob was brought into deeper fellowship with Him. The psalmist seems to be saying, "The same God who blessed Jacob in spite of all his rebellion and made him one of the patriarchs of the people of God—this God is our refuge!"

This divine affirmation assures us that our problems, even the ones we have deliberately caused, will not separate us from the Lord. He never gave up on Jacob and He will never give up on you or me. We can know and love Him and be still. He will exalt Himself in us. Our inner world will be at peace and our outer world be changed by His power. *The Living Bible* paraphrase of Psalm 94:14 puts it clearly, "The Lord will not forsake His people, for they are His prize." And that includes you and me!

After I finished writing this chapter and reclaimed for myself what I've tried to communicate to you, I pulled out again the biofeedback card I told you about. With new confidence I placed my thumb on the black square. Once again I counted to ten. Thank the Lord, it had turned blue—the blessed blue of inner calm!

4

WHEN
OUR HEARTS
ARE BROKEN

I HAVE A GREAT OLD FRIEND who always asks me a very personal, penetrating question when I see him. There's profound love in his voice and an encouraging twinkle in his eye as he asks, "Lloyd, tell me, how's your heart?"

Now I know my friend is not inquiring about the condition of the physical pump of my cardiovascular system. He uses the word "heart" in the biblical, Hebrew meaning of the inner person, the intellect, emotions, and the will. In response, I am free to talk about my hurts and hopes, delights and disappointments. I share what God seems to be saying to me in my challenges and opportunities, in my failures and successes.

Then, when I've exposed what's been happening in my heart, I ask my friend about the condition of his heart. In his responses he is equally vulnerable and free with me.

After we've shared what's on our hearts, we pray for each other. The time together is always refreshing and liberating. I feel a new resiliency for what's ahead. Together my friend and I pray for the Lord to continue to live in our hearts and to keep them sensitive, supple, and flexible.

How's Your Heart?

You and I have been endowed with the heart's ability to hope and dream. With the power of intellect we can set our goals and make plans for what we want our life to be. These purposes then become the focus of our heart's capability, desire, and determination. We develop a vision for our life, people, and what we want to accomplish.

But sometimes things don't work out the way we dreamed they should. People don't measure up and tend to disappoint us. Our carefully planned projects fail or are delayed for an excruciatingly long period of time. Sickness slows us up. Life's reversals distress us. Professional difficulties keep us from the salary or the job we've always wanted.

Added to our own problems are those being faced by the people in our lives. Since we have hopes and dreams for them, their problems hit us with full force. We want them to be happy, to succeed, and to live a full life. When life becomes difficult for them, the quakes in their lives are registered on the Richter scale of our own hearts.

Through all these traumatic bruises on our hearts' desires something happens inside us. We are hurt. Repeated hurts build up a resistance to being vulnerable to future hurts. Our hearts become dry and crisp, hardened by the external pressures of life. Like earth layers pressed and compacted over the centuries into stone, our hearts become hardened to life.

The Problem of Broken Hearts

So many of those who responded to my inquiry about life's biggest problems shared the problem of broken hearts. It was their way of expressing the grief they were feeling. Their hearts were broken by the death of loved ones, by the failures of life, or by what the difficulties of living had done to scuttle their fondest hopes for their life.

What can we do when problems break our hearts? There are few questions more crucial for us to ask and answer. And the answer, given in one of the most powerful promises of God, reveals what He wants to do in our hearts, what He offers us, and how that becomes the secret for resiliency to make life a constant succession of new beginnings. Two promises, one in Jeremiah and the other in Ezekiel, congeal into one vibrant promise from God for the problem of a broken heart.

The promise in Jeremiah was given when the hearts of the people of Israel were broken by the fall and destruction of Jerusalem. At that time many of the leaders and people were carried off into exile in Babylon. This was the result of sin and rebellion against the Lord. They had hardened their hearts against Him. And yet, He gave them this promise, "Then I will give them a heart to know Me, that I am the Lord; and they shall be My people, and I will be their God, for they shall return to Me with their whole heart" (Jer. 24:7).

In the second promise in Ezekiel the Lord explains how He will create this new heart-desire in His people. This promise was given during the same exile in Babylon. "Then I will give them one heart, and I will put a new spirit within them, and take the stony heart out of their flesh, and give them a heart of flesh, that they may walk in My statutes and keep My judgments and do them; and they shall be My people, and I will be their God" (Ezek. 11:19–20).

God Promises a Three-part Gift

These two promises from the Old Testament offer us a three-part gift when our hearts are broken by life's problems. First, we are prepared for a spiritual heart transplant; second, we are given a new heart; and, third, we are offered a fresh start. Our hearts are broken open at a deeper level to receive the Lord's heart.

1. We are prepared for a spiritual heart transplant. First, let's consider how a broken heart brings us into deeper fellowship with the Lord. He graciously invades our hearts with a desire to know Him. Problems do that to us. They break us open at one level of our hearts so that we discover how hard our hearts have become at the core. The immediate problem making our hearts ache reveals to us how closed we have become to the Lord and the overtures of His Spirit in our thinking, feeling, and willing.

Our imperious self-management of our hearts is exposed. We can't imagine how the Lord could have allowed this problem which impedes our plans and purposes. We have used the heart's endowments of intellect, emotion, and will to try to run our own lives and determine our own destiny. Was Oscar Wilde right? "How else but through a broken heart may Lord Christ enter in?"

Before we answer Wilde's question, let's reflect on some of the things that break our hearts.

Take our failures, for example. When we've blown it in some area we ache with self-incrimination and condemnation. But what was the deeper cause of the failure? Did we seek and follow guidance? Was the failure caused by willful disobedience to what we knew was right? Life's failures can either harden us to future help from the Lord or they can bring us to a realization of our human weaknesses and our need for His forgiveness and His strength for the future.

And what about the unfulfilled dreams that break our hearts? We set our purposes and plans and want God to bless them. When things don't work out, we question our carefully predetermined plans. Suddenly we long for God to help us in the future. This surface cracking open of our hearts leads us to realize how hard our hearts have become.

Then consider the people-problems that distress us. A broken relationship, a disappointment over a person's behavior, or our anguish over what they are doing to themselves or others (and us!) finally brings us to prayer about them. We are forced to surrender them to the Lord. Now, the inner core of our hearts is broken open to His guidance and power. We are given a new attitude of love and patience toward the people who trouble us.

But what about the losses of life that break our hearts with grief? The Lord certainly understands our pain, but He wants to give healing at a deeper level. Has something or someone become more important to us than Him? For example, the healing of the grief over the death of a loved one begins when we can tell the Lord how we are feeling and ask Him for His comfort and strength to endure. Then we are broken open at an even deeper level of our hearts. We gain the Lord's wisdom in our thinking, His peace in our emotions, and the acceptance of His will in our wills. We can praise the Lord for the person we've lost and the years we've enjoyed with him or her, claim that death is not an ending but a transition in eternal life.

I talked to a man who was on the edge of experiencing this gift of a heart truly open to God. He had lost his sixteen-year-old son. "I'm really angry at God for doing this!" he said. "How could He take this boy from me? He was a fine boy, believed in God, and had a great future. Now he's gone."

The man had three problems: the loss of his beloved son and the grief that was causing, the anger he was feeling that was blocking him from receiving the only source of comfort to endure the pain, and he was belaboring false assumptions that this life is the best of all lives and that his son was being denied a long life here. The man had not allowed himself to consider the blessing of heaven or the peace his son knew with our Lord. He was thinking only of himself and his loss. His plans for his lad would not be accomplished. He had planned to have him take over his business. Most of all, the man was aching over the denial of his enjoyment of his son. Very human reactions. But beneath all the grief was a hardened, self-determining will that had been threatened. Though the man claimed to be a Christian, he had never yielded the core of his heart to the Lord.

The bright side of the story is that the Lord did not leave the man to muddle in his grief forever. I did all that I could to help him to talk and cry out his grief and to gently clarify his thinking about death and eternal life. One day I felt led to say, "My friend, the Lord is going to give you a burning desire to open your heart to Him. He knows your grief. He gave His own Son to deal with the problem of death and to open heaven to us. I promise you that before long you will realize you can't make it without Him. That will open you to receive what He has been longing to give you. You are angry with God because you think He cancelled your plans."

Some days later the man suddenly felt differently inside. He was gripped by an undeniable desire to surrender his grief, confess how tenaciously he had held his own life and those he loved in his control. The Lord broke open the citadel of his heart and flooded it with His peace.

2. We are given a new heart. That account helps us to understand the second aspect of how the Lord deals with our broken hearts: He replaces our hardened heart with a new heart. His promise to Ezekiel contrasts a stony heart with a heart of flesh. A stony heart is one hardened by willfulness. A heart of flesh is just the opposite. "Flesh" throughout the Scriptures means our humanity. In this instance, the word means we will be given a human heart. That is, we will accept our humanity and let God be the Lord of our hearts. A stony heart is a heart seeking to play God over ourselves, our destiny, and the people of our lives. A fleshly heart is a feeling, flexible, free heart. Our intellect is yielded to think God's thoughts, our emotions become a channel of His Spirit of love, joy, peace. The will recovers its original purpose to implement the Spirit-guided thoughts and decisions of the Lord through our thinking brain.

This promise of God given to the people of Israel in Babylon that they would be given a new heart and a new Spirit to fill it was ultimately fulfilled through Christ's death, resurrection, and infilling of His people at Pentecost. When Christ died for us, Satan's power over us was broken. When we accept Christ's atoning death and experience the liberating power of His resurrection, we're prepared to receive His Spirit as our new heart. His love for us breaks open our hearts at the

deepest levels. He pulverizes our stony hearts. And it is as
we accept our humanity and yield our minds, emotions, and
wills to Him, that we receive a new heart. We are given a
new purpose, new plans, new power, and a new sensitivity
for the people in our lives.

3. *We are offered a fresh start.* Now we are ready to talk
about what happens with our attitude toward the future. With
a new, Christ-indwelt heart, we are able to deal with problems.
Instead of defeating us, they break us open to His guidance
and we can see them as the first stage of new beginnings.
We are able to say, "Well, Lord, what are You seeking to do
through this problem to prepare me for the next step in Your
strategy for me?" Life is made up of a constant succession
of new beginnings when Christ reigns in our hearts. We are
never totally defeated. He has a way through and out of the
problems and on to the next phase of our adventure with
Him. He gives us guidance of how to begin again. He never
gives up on us, and He gives us the courage and strength
never to give up on life.

Now we can cut the losses of our past failures and move
on. Having made a fresh start we have the strength to forgive
ourselves and others. When people have caused our broken
heart, He shows us how to express forgiveness. We are freed
from having to be right or win every argument. All that's
important to us is a new beginning. In response to other people's pain and distress, we feel deeply with the Lord's love
pulsating through our hearts for them. But we are never immobilized by their problems. We know from our own experience
that the Lord will use the problems to break open their hearts
to Him and to the future He has prepared. And finally, in
our own grief over loss of loved ones or cherished projects,
the Lord is the indwelling healer. We can express our grief,
let it out without blaming Him, and experience the miraculous
shifting of our feelings from the loss to what the Lord has
ahead for us.

Now, in the light of that, how's your heart? Has life

hardened it? Have you allowed experience to make it dry, crisp, and hard?

When problems break our hearts we are in a strategic place spiritually. We have the blessed opportunity of allowing the Lord to take charge of our hearts, break into the core of our self-determination, and set us free to receive His heart in us. The result will be a vibrant resiliency for the new beginning He has planned for us.

5

THE LAW OF MULTIPLYING RETURNS

IN THE EIGHTEENTH CENTURY, an economist by the name of Turgot established what he called the law of diminishing returns. Stated simply, he reasoned that an overinvestment of capital or labor results in a diminished profit.

For example, in a business, a certain amount of capital is needed for raw materials, facilities, and labor to produce, package, and distribute a product. Once a selling price is established in the competitive market, any unnecessary or excessive investment for production eventually lessens the profit. The overinvestment really becomes counter-productive to the ultimate purpose of making a profit.

The Law of Multiplying Returns

Seventeen centuries before Turgot, Jesus proclaimed a spiritual law that is just the opposite. It is the law of multiplying returns. We find the basis for that law in Luke's telling of the Sermon on the Mount, where Christ says: "Therefore be merciful, just as your Father also is merciful. Judge not, and you shall not be judged. Condemn not, and you shall not be condemned. Forgive, and you will be forgiven. Give, and it will be given to you: good measure, pressed down, shaken together, and running over will be put into your bosom. For with the same measure that you use, it will be measured back to you" (Luke 6:36–38).

From this we see that we are called into partnership with the Lord to live a merciful, nonjudgmental and noncondemnatory, giving and forgiving, generous life. That's the product. And to produce that through us, the Lord lavishes us with an overabundance of His grace because He wants us to emulate His own generous heart. We can't outgive the Lord. The more we give away of what He has entrusted to us, the more He invests in us. He's willing to overinvest in us because we are His strategy for communicating His generosity to the world.

A Mirthful Metaphor

The law of multiplying returns is vividly portrayed in Jesus' mirthful metaphor of overflowing blessing, ". . . good measure, pressed down, shaken together, and running over will be put into your bosom. . . ." Now, I'm going to use a bit of "sanctified imagination," and suggest what I think might have been in Jesus' mind when He used this metaphor of generosity.

This is the picture I see. The Palestinian sun is setting over a field that has just been harvested by the combined efforts of a landowner and his laborers. Tired, sweaty, and weary after days of harvesting the grain, the servants gather around the master to receive their pay for their hard labor in planting, cultivating, and harvesting the wheat. Months before, they had held bushel baskets for the master to fill with seed for the planting. Now they hold the same measures to be filled with the harvested and threshed grain. An equal measure is their due reward for their efforts.

The servants are wearing long, loose-fitting, sheathlike garments made of coarse material which extend down to their feet. Around their waists are ropelike girdles or belts. But now we see that the servants have pulled up the material above the belt, and formed a large pocket on their chests. Since there are no other pockets in their laborer's garb, this newly formed pocket above their waists is especially important to them. Each servant arranges his pocket to make it as large as possible.

The air is festive with the celebration of harvest. They had all worked hard. Master and servants were now friends because of their labor together. Now they could enjoy the results of their work. And the master knows that his servants are deserving of their wages.

Thankful for the bountiful harvest, the master lifts sack after sack of grain and fills his servants' bushel baskets to the top. But then when that is done, he still wants them to have more. So he pours more grain into their baskets until they overflow.

"Ah, that's still not enough!" the master says, his voice filled with laughter. Now he presses down the grain in the baskets to make room for more. It is a treasured moment of mutual affirmation. Now the master lifts all of the bushels, shaking them vigorously so that there will be more room for still more grain. On top of the compacted grain, he pours more. Again it spills over on the ground.

Even with that, the master's generosity has not found sufficient expression. Now he notices the empty pockets formed on the servant's chests from the folds of their robes. And with a twinkle in his eye he begins filling the pockets full as well. The servants, sensing the master's joy, join in the merriment and pull more of the material of their garments above their girdles to provide even bigger pockets which the master immediately fills to overflowing.

And then in a final expression of shared celebration, the master takes handfuls of grain and showers the servants with it, tossing some in their hair and pouring still more down the back of their necks.

Everyone feels a great sense of joy and satisfaction. Their job is finished for now, but it won't be long before the servants will work for the master again on the next project. They are important to his strategy, and they are dependent on his provision.

I'm convinced that something like that drama suggested Jesus' metaphor. The words "running over will be put into your bosom" prompted my thought about what might have been the basis of His impelling word-picture. The word "bosom," which in some translations is rendered "heart," is *kolpos* in the Greek text. It really means pocket. Since there were no pockets in laborers' garments worn in the field, I agree with many interpreters that what is meant is the pocket formed above the waist that I've described.

What I think Jesus was saying in this metaphor was not only an equal or even pressed down, overflowing bushel basket, but in addition, a filled up, spilling over pocket. That's the way God is with us. He wants us to overflow with His grace. The more we use of what He invests in us, the more He desires to give.

Action Steps

Let's reflect further on the implied progression of Jesus' metaphor ". . . give and it will be given to you. . . ." Give what? Note what precedes the admonition. "Therefore be merciful, just as your Father is also merciful. Judge not, and you shall not be judged. Condemn not, and you shall not be condemned. Forgive, and you will be forgiven" (Luke 6:36–37). All these are action steps in the application of generous love about which Jesus has been teaching in the passage as a whole. Now the metaphor becomes vividly clear. We are given a measure full of the Lord's mercy, grace, forgiveness, and care. When we reproduce that quality of love in our relationships

and responsibilities, we are not only replenished in equal,
but in overflowing, measure.

Two stages of blessing are implied. First comes recognition
of how much we have received of the Lord's provision, His
providential care and love and forgiveness through the Cross.
That prompts us to respond in faith and the commitment of
our lives. A new life in Christ begins. But it's when we begin
to share what we have received that we discover the secret
of infilling power. Then we realize that the overflowing grain
of Jesus' metaphor is really His own Spirit. And there's no
limit of what He wants to give us of Himself.

What would you say is the distinguishing quality of a truly
alive, dynamic Christian? Great faith, sound convictions, im-
peccable character? No, I think it's generosity: the freedom
to receive and give unqualified, nonmanipulative love. And
for that we must discover how to receive graciously. What
the Lord wants from us He gives to us in abundance. This
is what I believe Jesus is saying in this mirthful metaphor
of generosity. And we need generosity to combat one of our
greatest problems—that of selfishness.

A Promise for the Problem of Selfishness

Many people have told me that they believe selfishness is
the number one problem facing us today. But most of the
time we don't see it as our problem—it applies to *other* people.

And yet, selfishness, the inordinate concern for ourselves,
is a problem we all face at times. Some people, most of the
time. Growing out of an inadequate experience of grace, we
are fearful there won't be enough of life's blessings to go
around. So we measure everything in terms of what's happening to us, what we get, and what we must demand for our
security and satisfaction. Our concern is whether we got what
was coming to us and whether or not people are paying attention to us. Selfishness is not self-love, but an aching lack of
experiencing the Lord's gracious love for us.

In our selfishness we get caught up in a power struggle to try to gain and keep control over ourselves, others, and even God. We become defensive of our turf and want to impress our wills on other people. We want what we want when we want it.

Some time ago a friend of mine called me long-distance to share his disappointment over being bypassed for a key position as head of his department in a large corporation in the Middle West. After the shock of not receiving the promotion he'd been working for for years, he had sublimated his anger with a determination to keep control of the department even though someone else would be in charge.

"It doesn't make any difference who's in charge, just so I'm still in control!" my friend said.

"Sounds like you're heading for a no-win power struggle," I cautioned.

"Maybe so," my friend responded, "but no one knows this department better than I do and I'm not about to lose all the effort and hard work I've put in building it up over the years. I don't really care who has the title—just so I still can call the shots."

My friend's frankness was shocking. It also revealed his selfishness. But I hear the same battle for power in husbands and wives who are in deadly struggle for control. Parents express it about children who threaten their control. People feel it about friends who dare to resist their forceful manipulation. Churches are often rendered ineffective by individuals and groups seeking to dominate.

But the lust for control is not just the problem of the more obvious power brokers. It's in all of us. Our struggle for control eventually blocks the flow of power from the Lord. But He is able to bless those who put their lives under His control.

I know people who are in a power struggle with God. Then there are those who are struggling to gain His power for their own purposes. Both of these are losers. The winners are those who surrender their control over to the Lord's control. Only as we do that can we participate in the law of multiplying returns.

Stingy Receivers

One of the great causes of selfishness is our reluctance to receive the blessings the Lord offers us. We are stingy receivers! But He doesn't give up.

How does the Lord deal with selfishness? Does He take away what we have to shock us awake to our self-centered attitudes? Sometimes. But most often He employs the law of multiplying returns. He knows our problem is one of learning how to give ourselves away generously. And so He melts our icy hearts with the warmth of His goodness, rather than smash us with condemnatory judgment. Often He uses the very problems we experience to show us His faithfulness, and His consistent interventions finally convince us of the limitless generosity of His heart. The Lord knows He finally has gotten through to us when we come to the place of wanting to be as generous with others as He has been to us. But in order to do that we need power. And that's exactly what the Lord offers to provide.

Our Real Purpose

The Lord's power is given for the accomplishment of His purposes. That's the secret of His law of multiplying returns. He wants to make us like Himself.

In Matthew's version (5:43–48) of the same portion of the Sermon on the Mount we've been considering in Luke, the Master concludes His teaching on the generous life with a mind-boggling promise which expresses the metaphor of over-flowing blessing in another way.

After Jesus had described the generous life exemplified by God's mercy, forgiveness, and love, He challenged His follow-ers with their awesome purpose—"that you may be sons of your Father" (Matt. 5:45). As daughters and sons we are to express our family likeness to the Father by loving extravagantly as He has loved us. Then Jesus promised, "Therefore you shall be perfect, just as your Father in heaven is perfect" (Matt. 5:48). That word "perfect" causes us to stop and think. How can we be perfect as our heavenly Father is perfect?

A deeper understanding of the Greek word used for "perfect" is very revealing. It means "end," "goal," or "purpose." In other words, something is perfect in this sense when it accomplishes the purpose for which it was formed. A person is perfect when he or she expresses the purpose for which he or she was created. An added implication of the word means "complete," "mature."

What Jesus seems to be saying here is, "You shall accomplish the purpose for which you were created, even as your Father in heaven accomplishes His purpose." But, the more I have studied the meaning of this promise, the more I have come to believe that Jesus' intention can be expressed this way, "You shall accomplish your purpose because it is your heavenly Father's purpose to aid you in accomplishing that purpose."

Power for Our Purpose

Here is the gospel in summary: Christ came to reveal that the Father's essential purpose for us is to accept His love and in response to seek and do His will. Throughout His incarnate life on earth, Jesus taught that surrender and obedience are the keys to receiving the Father's power. And he lived what He taught. His watchword was, "Not My will, but Yours be done." His constant prayer was "Abba, Father!"—the intimate words of trust meaning simply "dearest Father." He taught us to pray "our Father." There was never any question in His mind or heart about who was in charge or in control. He modeled life without a power struggle and lived a life emulating the nature and character of the Father. His unequaled love, the works He accomplished, and the miracles He performed—all exemplified His complete trust in and obedience to God the Father. In the Garden of Gethsemane and on the cross the word in His heart and on His lips was *Father*.

The Father's Unlimited Investment

Christ died on the cross to set us free from the bondage of sin—the sin of rebellion against the Father, the refusal to be His obedient sons and daughters, the selfishness which stands in the way of loving as He has loved us. The cross was not only a forgiveness of sin but a cosmic defeat of Satan's hold over us.

Having won that battle, Christ was raised from the dead. The empty tomb was the Father's vindication of Christ's atoning death on the cross. And after the resurrection and ascension the Father again sent the Son to continue what He had begun. Paul puts this in stirring words, "And because you are sons, God has sent forth the Spirit of His Son into your hearts, crying out, 'Abba, Father!' " (Gal. 4:6). The indwelling Christ is the One who gives us the power for our purpose— to be merciful, forgiving, nonjudgmental, accepting children of the Father. What we could never do on our own, He gives us the will to do. We cannot meet the Father's absolute demand of our obedience without Christ's enabling help. He does not promise to meet all our surface needs on our demand, but demands that we face that our deepest need is to obey. Christianity is a Father movement and His presence with us in Christ is to press us forward in realizing our full potential. We desperately need the Father's call to excellence, forgiveness when we fail, and encouragement to begin again.

The absence of strong teaching and preaching of the Father today has left Christians to wallow in subjectivity. There's little emphasis on the Father's holiness, purity, and judgment. That makes life a trial without a judge. We are guided by cultural values, confused about morality, and self-indulgent in satisfying our own desires. We are missing Father in the church, the household of faith. We need His bracing, character-building demands that we be all He created us to be. When we admit that our lives are out of control as long as we maintain our selfish control, then His powerful presence with and in us in Christ makes us able to press on in His purpose for us.

Now we can see how both Jesus' metaphor of overflowing blessing and His promise that we shall be perfect just as our heavenly Father is perfect, blend together as the basis of the law of multiplying returns. What God demands from us He develops in us; what He requires He releases in bountiful measure; what He decides, He provides. Our God is one Lord—eternal, sovereign and enabling Savior, challenging Father and comforting Friend. We are never left to try to make it on our own.

He Is Able!

The "pressed down, shaken together, running over" quality of Christ's power is triumphantly expressed by six "He is able" affirmations in the New Testament. The joy that pulsates from the writers of the Scriptures is not "we are able!" but "Christ is able!" The Greek word for "able" comes from *dunamis*, "power." This is what the all-sufficient Christ is able to do for us.

Paul writes:

> "Now to Him who is able to do exceedingly abundantly above all that we ask or think, according to the power that works in us" (Eph. 3:20).
> ". . . for I know whom I have believed and am persuaded that He is able to keep what I have committed to Him until that Day" (2 Tim. 1:12).
> ". . . He is able to subdue all things to Himself" (Phil. 3:21).

The author of Hebrews writes:

"For in that He Himself has suffered, being tempted, He is able to aid those who are tempted" (Heb. 2:18).
"Therefore He is also able to save to the uttermost those who come to God through Him, since He ever lives to make intercession for them" (Heb. 7:25).

And Jude writes:

"Now to Him who is able to keep you from stumbling, and to present you faultless before the presence of His glory with exceeding joy" (Jude 24).

What a marvelous crescendo of "He is able" assurances is found in these words! Christ is able to give us power beyond our ability to ask or deserve. He is able to intervene to help us in what we commit to His care. He is able to overcome the problems which threaten to defeat us and to give us strength when we are tempted to miss His best for us. He is able to make us whole by healing our spiritual, physical, emotional, and circumstantial needs. And He is able to forgive all our sins and mistakes and accept us as if we had never failed in the first place. We are not left alone to struggle for power; we are given more than we need. Why? Because the Lord wants to use us as part of His overflowing blessing in the lives of others.

The Power to Bless

The Lord gives us power not to control others but to communicate what life can be for them under His control. That's why He is so generous—to show the world the overflowing sufficiency of a life placed under His absolute sovereignty. When we accept that, our leadership and influence will be impelling. We cannot "lord it over" people and still communicate the grace of the Lord to them. But to empower us to share His grace the Lord overinvests in us for a multiplying return.

A Perfect Ten

I especially enjoyed the gymnastic events in the 1984 Olympic Games. After watching each of the athletes perform, I waited expectantly with the crowd for the rating from one to ten on the Longines rating meter, which indicated the combined scores of the judges. I was intrigued by the method of scoring—each athlete began with a ten. It was lack of skill that lowered the score.

This gymnastic scoring procedure prompted me to think about what a perfect ten would be for me in the use of Christ's superabundant power to love generously. Then I thought of ten generous aspects of His grace He wants to give me to love, care, and serve others. When I can place a score of one beside any of them on any day, I know I've succeeded in fulfilling my purpose of being part of the law of multiplying returns. Here's what I think an overflowing blessing of His love is like. It is:

> Unlimited in its source
> Unmotivated by its recipient
> Unbounded in its expression
> Unqualified in its acceptance
> Unreserved in its affirmation
> Unstinting in its forgiveness
> Unconditional in its initiative efforts
>   for reconciliation
> Unfailing in its empathy
> Untiring in its involvement
> Unrelenting in its persistence

Place a one before the aspects of Christ's grace you've been open to receive from Him. Now add up the total of His investment in you. It is reassuring to know that we start each day with a ten!

Now, go back over the list. Place a one before those which others might say characterize your use of what you have received from the Lord in your relationship with them. Now compare the two totals. Is there any difference? If so, you have your marching orders for the next steps toward your purpose of emulating the generous heart of the Lord.

When we reflect on the law of multiplying returns we are left to wonder why we struggle for power if indeed Christ's power has been entrusted to us. Why do we wrestle with life and hold it with such a tight grip?

It's to that problem and to another of Christ's exciting promises that we turn our attention in the next chapter. We're going to build on what we've discovered so far about the law of multiplying returns. The further secret awaiting us is the amazing paradox of power: We can only give away what we have, and we can keep only what we give away.

6

LOSING YOUR GRIP ON LIFE

A FRIEND OF MINE who was facing what seemed to be insurmountable problems in several important areas of his life shared a frightening dream he had had every night for weeks. "I guess I'm losing my grip on life," he said.

He dreamed that he was in a fast-moving river and was paddling against the current while holding on to a life preserver that kept him afloat. While clutching the buoyant float, he tried desperately to swim back up the river. And yet, the harder he swam, the more difficult it became to buck the irreversible force of the surging current.

When I asked my friend to describe the river more fully, he remembered an amazing thing. At one end of the river, from which he had been carried by the force of the currents, was a dark, forbidding cloud. At the other end he could see from a distance was a bright, beautiful sky with a rainbow arched over it.

Now, I'm no Joseph or Daniel when it comes to interpreting

dreams. Nor am I a skilled psychoanalyst in plumbing the depths of dream analysis. And yet, the meaning of this dream seemed so obvious, and so perfectly matched to the man's spiritual condition, that I decided to gently press him to think through what the Lord and his inner heart were trying to communicate to him. Dreams often are the focus of what our subconscious mind is trying to tell us. They also can be what our conscious minds resist recognizing in our waking hours. And dreams can be a way the Lord uses to get through to us. In this case, I was convinced that all three things were happening.

"What do you think the dark cloud and the bright, rainbow-arched sky at the ends of the river represent?" I asked.

In response to my question, my friend said thoughtfully, "Well, that dark, forbidding cloud must mean something bad. Like a storm or difficulty. And the rainbow-filled sky must be something good. I can remember as a boy in Sunday school I was told that the rainbow in the Old Testament was a sign of the covenant, a reassurance of God's blessing on His people."

Then he smiled and added, "Why didn't I see that before? The one end of the river is difficulty and frustration, the other end is blessing!"

Suddenly his face darkened and furrowed into a perplexed frown. "The currents of the river are carrying me toward blessing. Yet I'm swimming against that tide. I hang on to the life preserver and try to swim back to the dark end of the river. Sometimes in the dream, I take markings along the side of the river. There seems to be a halfway point between the cloud and the rainbow, and I try to stay there, halfway between the two."

"What do you think that life preserver is?" I asked, hardly able to contain my excitement over what I was convinced the Lord was trying to get across.

He paused for what seemed to be a long time. "Well, it keeps me afloat. I never have the fear of drowning in my dreams. And yet I use it to fight my way back to the cloud rather than floating on to the rainbow."

As he said that the frown lifted from his face. "The only thing that has kept me afloat in this troubled time of my life is my faith in Christ. So, I guess that life preserver is my faith."

And then he said, "The Lord has kept me afloat in that river, but He's trying to move me on. I keep trying to go back to my old life of worry and fear rather than allowing the currents to press me on to the blessing the Lord has for me. Wow, that seems absurd, doesn't it?—using my faith just to stay afloat and not go forward. But, you know, each time I awake I have the feeling I'll never win against those currents. Even with one arm in the life ring and one arm thrashing against the currents to stay where I am, I'll not be able to hold my position for long. And if it's a blessing that rainbow-arched sky holds, why should I try?"

"Why indeed?" I replied. I knew it was time to tie that dream, and the revelation of insight it had provided, to some solid, objective truth in the promises of the Master. I selected one that had become very real to me in a similar point of growth in my own relationship with Christ. He had not used a dream to get through to me, but the liberating realization was no less impelling or exciting.

"My friend, you are on the edge of realizing the truth of one of Christ's greatest promises!"

"Really?" he said, "Tell me, I don't want to have that frustrating dream again."

I opened my Bible and read Matthew 10:39: "He who finds his life will lose it, and he who loses his life for My sake will find it." Then I turned to Matthew 16:25 for another expression of that same basic truth, "For whoever desires to save his life will lose it, and whoever loses his life for My sake will find it."

What I shared with my friend that day is the subject of this chapter.

When Losing Your Grip Is a Blessing

So many people these days tell me that their biggest problem is that they are losing their grip on life. But what we think is a problem is really a momentous sign of growth.

The title of this chapter is meant to be a double-entendre—a title with two meanings. What we think is a problem is really a blessing. We feel we are losing our grip on controlling people, circumstances, and the future. But the promise Christ gives us about finding and losing life is that when we lose our grip on life we are on the way to discovering the secret of the more abundant life He longs to give us.

The river of fast-moving currents in my friend's dream provides us a vivid biblical context for understanding Jesus' promise. Repeatedly in the Scriptures, the river of life is a metaphor used to exemplify the flow of God's Spirit giving new life and for carrying His people on to the plan and purposes He has for them. We can understand what the Lord was trying to tell my friend, and us, when we realize that the endless, irrevocable flow of the Lord's gracious care issues from the headwaters of His heart and flows through history into our time. They are currents of self-giving and sacrificial love. The Lord gave Himself in creating us to receive His love, in coming to prepare us to be riverbeds for the flow of the life-giving water of life in His Incarnation. He is the relentless giver of love, forgiveness, and daily strength, and Calvary is the flood-gate through which that life-giving water flows. It cannot be stopped up or drained off into a pollutable eddy.

Now, to become a Christian is to step into that river. It is meant to carry us into fullness of blessing and power. Why then are we so reluctant to enjoy the moving currents pulling us on to a more abundant life? Is it because, like my friend, we fight against the current as we try to keep afloat in the midst of problems instead of realizing that the very problems we face are used by the Lord to carry us on to further realization of His purpose for us?

But before we become too metaphorical and allegorical, let's look at what Jesus meant in His pithy, paradoxical promise about finding and losing life and tie that down to our practical experience in living with daily problems. There are two stages of growth in this amazing promise. First, "He who finds his life will lose it," and second, "He who loses his life for My sake will find it." That tells us how Christ helps us begin to live the abundant life and then how to receive its full potential. Both are crucial for facing life's problems.

To Give or to Keep?

Salient, powerful spiritual and psychological truths are inherent in Jesus' promise. *We can only give away what we have, and we can keep only what we give away.* Let's take these mighty maxims in the order of their progression to learn how the Lord calls us and then enlists us in His plan and purposes.

We can only give away what we have. The Lord begins with us by first giving us a life of value so we can in turn give it back to Him. His initial work in our minds is to communicate to us our value to Him. The gospel begins, and never ends, in the eternal assurance of His love for us and of our value to Him. Through Christ we receive the giving, forgiving, gracious heart of God. This marvelous truth is fortified by a promise in Revelation 7:17 that tells us of the life-giving ministry of the Savior: "For the Lamb who is in the midst of the throne will shepherd them and lead them to living fountains of waters. And God will wipe away every tear from their eyes." The term "midst of the throne" does not imply geographical or spacial distance. The Lord is with us. His task is to convince us of His love, our worth to Him, and to give us a new self-understanding, self-acceptance, and self-esteem.

Over the years, from my own experience in my own life and as one who has witnessed the birth of thousands of Christians, I have learned that it is a fine blend of honesty about ourselves and a realization of what we are missing that the Lord uses to bring a person through the spiritual birth canal into the new life. When we know that we are loved and confess that we can't make it on our own, we are freed to surrender our old life and step into the river of new life in Christ. Down-and-outer or up-and-outer go through the same process. We felt singled out, cherished, loved to the uttermost, forgiven when we didn't deserve it, and called to be the Lord's persons when we didn't think we had anything to offer. The Lord gave us a life to give Him. We exclaim that we found a new life, but more accurately, we were found by the Lord. Like in my friend's dream, the currents of the Lord's Spirit carried us downstream away from an old life with its dark, forbidding clouds of our own brand of sin, self-negation, and futility.

And then, somewhere along the way in our new-found joy in the currents, we awake to the realization that He has called us for a purpose. The same purpose exemplified in His self-giving, sacrificial, servant heart. We now see that life in Christ means sharing His love and forgiveness with others and caring about the needs of people He puts on our agenda. And we are meant to draw on resources He gives us for sharing the gospel with the world, and in becoming involved with human suffering. But it is at this point that many of us began thrashing around in mid-stream halfway between our old life and the potential of a new life. We stepped into the river but were not sure we liked where it was carrying us.

We move now to the second truth in Jesus' promise: *We can keep only what we give away.* The joy of living is the delight of giving. There's no other way. Self-giving is not just based on the Lord's plan, or even on His will, but solidly rooted in His character. Outflowing love in specific acts of giving is not just what the Lord does, but what He is. He expects nothing less from us.

That means that if we are to do things the Lord's way, there is no other option, no other way to live. But there is a choice. Often. Every day. Usually repeatedly all through each day. And that's the essence of "losing our life" once we have found it. The more we give away of the life He has enabled us to find, the more we find of its joy, peace, and power. Everything we have and are now belongs to Him. And the more we give out, the more the Lord can put in. When we lose *our* grip on life, we experience His "forever-grip" on us.

That's why I've used "losing your grip on life" as a double-entendre, a statement that can mean two things. When we feel we are losing our grip, we probably need to lose it. Holding on to life is a sure way to miss its joy.

The Conservation Problem

We all experience what I call the conservation problem. The positive meaning of the word implies preservation, to keep from loss, decay, waste, or injury. Conservation can be a good thing when it comes to preserving our nation's natural resources or maintaining the God-entrusted values which gave birth to and have sustained our nation. I'm a "conservative" when it comes to conserving the basics of the faith—the divine inspiration of the Scriptures, the Lordship of Christ, the substitutionary sacrifice of the cross for the sins of the world, the gift of faith as the only basis of a right relationship with the Lord, and absolute necessity of receiving His indwelling Spirit to live the new life.

The negative side of conservation is that it can make us overly cautious. We can spend so much time conserving our faith that we resist communicating it to others. We become hoarders. Intent on preservation we miss our calling of propagation. As we stressed in the previous chapter, we forget that the Lord wants to replenish His grace in us constantly so we will have an overflowing blessing for the people around us. It is when we close the outflow of His love to others that conservation becomes a problem.

What I'm driving at can be illustrated by the experience I had with a trust. Many years ago, I established an Ogilvie

Family Trust for the education of my three children. A lawyer friend of mine became the trustee, or conservator, of the trust. He took the money I placed in the trust and creatively invested it so it would be maximized for when the children needed it. Now, if he had become so preoccupied with building up the funds that he refused to grant the children's requests for their educational bills, he would have denied the purpose of the trust. I'm happy he did not say, "Sorry, your education will have to wait. The money is drawing high returns now. Call me in a few years and I'll think about helping you then. But don't forget—this money is to be saved and built up, not to be squandered." Instead, when Heather, Scott, and Andrew called, his response was, "Why, of course. That's what the money is for. What do you need?"

Sometimes we react in a clutching way as the trustees of the spiritual and material blessings the Lord has entrusted to us. We deny the stipulations of our holy trust, and calling.

This problem of the wrong kind of conservation hits us all somewhere as we are being carried along by the currents of the Lord's Spirit. When was it for you? When did "the cost of discipleship," to use Dietrich Bonhoeffer's words, dawn on you? Chances are, you gripped your life ring of faith and began back-paddling against the currents. And while we were thrashing about, trying to keep from being carried out into the deeps, Jesus sounded in our souls, "He who finds his life will lose it."

The implication of "lose" here is not loss of our status as forgiven and loved people or of our faith as if it were a temporary gift which, like some object, could be lost never to be found again. Rather, I think the meaning here is to give away, or lose a selfish grip on it.

Losing and Finding Life

It is what we give up—what we lose—that makes possible what we receive from the Lord. So important is this truth to our lives and our ability to handle life's problems that Jesus amplified His earlier comments on "losing and finding" in Matthew 10:38–39 with these words, "If anyone desires to come after Me, let him deny himself, and take up his cross, and follow Me. For whoever desires to save his life will lose it, and whoever loses his life for My sake will find it. For what is a man profited if he gains the whole world, and loses his own soul? Or what will a man give in exchange for his soul?" (Matt. 16:24–26).

The setting of the latter words of Jesus followed Peter's bold confession that He was the Christ, the Messiah. The Lord then responded by telling Peter and the other disciples about the new life they would receive. He affirmed that they would be given the keys of the kingdom, and that they were called to be a new people, the church, the new Israel. And immediately after that Jesus talked about His death in Jerusalem and the assurance of the resurrection.

Peter responded to Jesus' mention of His death with consternation. He may have been wise enough to know that if that quality of sacrifice were to be required of the Master, it would also be required of him, as a disciple of Jesus. Peter had barely stepped into the river of a new life with his confession when he was resisting the currents of God's heart flowing through the Savior. To Peter's protest, "Far be it from You, Lord; this shall not happen to You!" Jesus responded sharply, "Get behind Me, Satan! You are an offense to Me, for you are not mindful of the things of God, but the things of men."

We can identify with Peter's concern for the Master—and for himself. Confrontation with the servant, suffering heart of God is a shock to us also. No sooner do we find ourselves than He calls us to self-giving. To take up our cross is not just some inconvenience, a bodily ailment, or a difficult person. Rather, it is denying ourselves the right to control our destiny and becoming involved in costly self-giving for the needs of others. It's death to self and resurrection to a new life of service. But the exchange rate is more than worth it.

Notice the play on the words "life" and "soul" in Matthew 16:25–26. We see from this how we give away the new life we have found as His gift to us determines the development of our eternal souls, that portion of us that lives forever.

Christ not only gives us a new, abundant life in the here and now, but He promises that how we use that gift of new life as an expression of our servanthood will determine the quality of soul we take into heaven. Because the character of God is outgoing love, and the whole program of heaven is initiative caring and sacrificial love, we would be very uncomfortable there if the major thrust in our lives on earth had not been to be servants. We'd be out of sync. Our preparation for heaven begins now. In fact, when we live life in Jesus' style, heaven begins now. And at the point of our physical death, all it can become is better, richer, fuller.

Giving and Growing

At this point you may be wondering what losing our lives has to do with our central theme of our problems and God's promises. Plenty. In fact, everything. All our problems have built into them an opportunity for a deeper experience of the self-sacrificing heart of the Lord. As we confront our problems, we must choose between being self-serving or self-sacrificing. We are on the way to a right choice when we can ask in the midst of a problem, "What does love command? How can I forget about my own selfish desires and think about what this troublesome person or that complex situation needs?" Remember, we are not in the abundant life to conserve ourselves, but to give ourselves away. And the more self-giving we are, the more we grow. Our character becomes more like Christ's.

For example, problems with people give us a splendid opportunity to reveal Christ's Spirit working through us as we show patience and are gracious and forgiving. At other times, His tenderness is coupled with toughness as we are called to take our stand for what He has shown us is right. Most people who become a problem to us are the way they are because they either need to meet the Savior or, if they have met Him, need to grow in Him. And His power is given to us for His program: to serve. A servant acts, speaks, gives, to communicate healing love and to help people find a life worth giving away.

The frustrating, disturbing things people do are because they are involved in their own rendition of trying to save rather than lose their lives. Like us, they need to lose their grip on life. And the secret of helping them let go is to communicate that they have a life of value to give. Problems with certain people are gifts from the Lord! It is because He has called, chosen, and cherished them that He allows them to become our problem. He wants to use us to expose what it means to find life and lose it for a new life filled with His Spirit.

The same is true for problematical situations which confront us. In each there's the choice of self-preservation or self-sacrificing service in Christ's name. He will show us exactly what we are to do and say as His servant. Obedience to that guidance is absolutely necessary.

A crucial way that we will be called to serve will be in the use of our material resources for the expansion of the kingdom and the alleviation of human suffering. I believe the Lord is in search of Christians whom He can trust to bless with financial blessings. He wants to get His work done through people who have lost their tight grip on life, including money.

Since our money is a congealed expression of ourselves, we can't lose ourselves without losing the acquisitive desire to conserve it for ourselves. Giving ourselves away to Christ means giving our money to the work of evangelism and world mission. He guides us to give through the church and para-church organizations that are actually reaching people with the good news of salvation through Christ and in caring for the hungry, lost, and disadvantaged of the world. Added to these more organized channels of our giving, the Lord gives us opportunities to give money or material assistance to individuals and families He brings to our attention.

I also believe that the biblical mandate for losing the life we've found is returning our tithe to the Lord. I've never met a joyous person living the abundant life to the fullest who isn't at least a tither—who knows that the first tenth of all that he or she receives belongs to the Lord. In fact, using the tithe for ourselves is embezzling God! It was never ours. Giving begins after we have expeditiously given our tithe in support of His work in the world.

Often the Lord allows financial problems to surface to bring us to the place of losing our grip on our money and material things. The first step to the solution of financial worries is to begin to tithe. That may seem absurd to those who are facing excruciating anxiety about financial pressures and shortages.

Recently a woman shared with me her panic over her family's financial problems. She and her husband had gone through a painful period of not being able to make ends meet. The husband's loss of a job for a long period and the illness of their son had drained all their resources.

Now, though her husband was back at work, they were struggling their way back to some measure of financial security. In spite of my emphasis on the importance of tithing, they had decided to wait to begin tithing until their backlog of bills were paid and they were back in shape financially. But their money problems persisted.

Finally in desperation one Sunday they both felt moved to begin tithing even though they were still hard pressed. It was the turning point. It wasn't long before the husband got a promotion and a raise in salary. Certain people who owed them money for a long time paid up. They started to pull out of their financial tailspin.

A success story? Yes, but only one of thousands I could tell. But sadly, there are an equal number of accounts I could relate of Christians who are financially secure, if not affluent, whose spiritual life is locked on dead-center because they have missed the secret that the joy of living is the delight of giving. Their reluctance to give their money courageously is only a sign of their resistance to give their whole lives to Christ. They are swimming against the tides of the currents of the flow of the Lord's self-giving love. They are trying to save themselves. For what? They conserve their energy and money, fearful that they might not have enough for their own needs. Stinginess in giving our money will not keep us out of heaven, but it will shrink and distort the quality of soul we take with us to heaven.

A Practical Perspective on Losing . . . and Finding Life

My friend whose dream I described at the opening of this chapter had all the kinds of problems we've discussed. His marriage was in trouble, he had difficulties at work, and was feeling a financial pinch. It was this montage of problems that had contributed to his dream of swimming against the currents. He had become a Christian several years before his recurring dream. At first his relationship with the Lord gave him a great joy and confidence. But it was all inflow and no outgo. His alarming dream opened him up to specific ways he had to let go of his grip on life and lose himself in the needs of others.

As we talked together about the troubled areas of his life we began with his marriage and identified specific ways he could express Christ's love for his wife. That meant listening to her needs rather than constantly telling her how she didn't meet his needs. Next, we made a list of things he could do to show his love for her. The list included everything from an adjusted work schedule so he could spend more time at home, to actually doing things around the house that his wife had been asking him to do for months.

Then we tackled his behavior on the job. He had a large staff reporting to him, and he had long treated them more like servants than people with needs. He was long on demands and short on encouragement. We talked about what it would mean to be the cheerleader for his staff. Some of them had personal needs which hindered their job performance. We discussed how he could help by listening to them and by caring for them. Again a list was drawn of specific steps for him to take.

The man had few close friends because he seldom shared his inner feelings and almost never asked anyone for help. In fact, his conversation with me about his dream was evidently the first time in years he had reached out to share a need with a friend.

Because of this phony front, no one ever felt free to reach out to him in friendship or talk with him about their needs. This, of course, explained why he had seldom talked about his faith. To overcome that, he made a list of people whom he knew needed Christ. And he then put feet to his list by deliberately seeking these people out, and witnessing to them in words and actions.

Finally, although the man made a good salary, he was living beyond his means and constantly scrambled to keep up with the bills. His donations to the church and a few community organizations were meager, and he ignored the biblical mandate of tithing.

This was probably the toughest change my friend tackled. But he agreed to tithe as an experiment. He opened a separate checking account for the deposit of the tenth of his salary checks. Then, from that account he began to write checks to the church, to certain strategic mission programs, and to people who were in financial need. He was amazed to discover that he still had more than enough to pay his own bills, and he began to enjoy the adventure of being a co-partner with the Lord.

I have told this story in such detail because it puts into

practical perspective how when we lose ourselves in Christ's program it releases His power in us. This sequence of events took place over two years ago. Today, he's a very different man than the worried person I first talked to about his dream.

Sure, he's still got problems. But now his problems are seen as a challenge, a new opportunity to lose the life he has newly found in Christ. As he began to think of himself as a servant, his relationships and his life were changed. His marriage has deepened. He claims to be more in love with his wife now than ever. People at work are functioning much more effectively. Instead of being feared for imperious methods of management, he's admired, and his employees are working harder than ever and enjoying it more. He has also become involved in sharing his faith with his friends and is active in the evangelism program of our church. When he led one of his first converts to Christ, it was one of the most exciting days of his life.

We shouldn't be surprised by the remarkable results of this man's decision to stop resisting the currents of the flow of the Lord's Spirit. He simply stopped resisting the Lord and got on His program. Self-giving is the order of any day—there's no other way!

The apostle Paul spoke to this truth in the Book of Romans. The first eleven chapters deal with God's gracious self-giving in Christ. With great detail Paul described the outpouring of God's love, forgiveness, new life, and power. Then, at the opening of chapter 12, he shared the secret of how to live in the flow of that love. What he wrote is really an explanation of Jesus' promise of how to find ourselves, lose ourselves, and then find life to the fullest: "I beseech you therefore, brethren, by the mercies of God, that you present your bodies a living sacrifice, holy, acceptable to God, which is your reasonable service. And do not be conformed to this world, but be transformed by the renewing of your mind, that you may prove what is that good and acceptable and perfect will of God" (Rom. 12:1–2).

The mercies of God Paul refers to are the source of all that we have and are. God has loved us and given Himself for us in Christ's life, death, and resurrection. And He is with us still through Christ's Spirit to provide us all we need to live life to the fullest. He has given us a new self to give over to His control. It is that life we are to sacrifice to the Lord. And when we live for Him by being channels of His giving and forgiving, serving and sacrificing love for others, our lives are consistent with His will and will overflow with lasting joy. We will be in harmony with His acceptable (effective, efficient) and perfect (accomplishing its purpose and end) will and plan for us.

Where are we in the river of new life? Swimming against the current of the Lord's plan or flowing with it? He wants to do more than just keep us afloat, while we resist the flow.

Ever feel you're losing your grip on life? Congratulations! Let go of your own grip. Grasp the cross. You are loved, cherished, valued. The Lord won't ever let go of you. Give your life to His control. He'll take it and give you back a more exciting, fulfilling life than you've ever known. Give your time to Him and He'll give you back eternity. Give yourself to people in need and He'll give you a heart overflowing with love. Give your money over to His management and He'll give you back more than you need.

I have a crusty old friend who's a real character. He has the ability to boil things down to bare essentials. What he lacks in grammar is more than made up by his wisdom and the color of his expression: "God ain't got no nobodies. He makes us somebody so He's got somebody He can use!"

7

FREEDOM FROM FRUSTRATION

As I SAT IN AN airport passenger check-in lounge waiting for
my flight to be called for boarding, I became aware of a drama
of frustration being played out by three people seated next
to me.

The characters in this drama were a "take charge" older
lady, her grandson Jimmy, and Jimmy's mother. The grandmother oozed with "mother hen" attention focused on Jimmy.
Her fondling affection revealed more of *her* need than the
boy's devotion to his grandmother. His obvious reluctance
to accept her smothering attention was expressed in his body
language—indicating more endurance than appreciation.

On the other side of the grandmother was Jimmy's mother,
a dutiful, but obviously exasperated daughter-in-law. The look
on her face clearly indicated that she was determined to remain
pleasant until the flight was called and her mother-in-law left.

The time of waiting was filled with the grandmother's final,
but somewhat imperious, instructions about how her daughter-
in-law should raise Jimmy, how she knew it would be difficult

without her help, and, how much he would miss her. Jimmy was asked several times if he loved Grandma, and if he would be a good boy until she returned for her next visit.

When the flight was called, grandmother gathered up all her packages, and with attention-getting flourishes, boarded the plane in a flood of tears.

After she was out of eyesight, Jimmy exclaimed, "Whew, I'm glad she's gone!"

Jimmy's mother's face flushed with a combination of embarrassment and consternation when she realized I had overheard the boy's honest expression of relief. Then she looked at Jimmy with a sternness. Even though it was obvious his childhood directness had expressed exactly how she was feeling, she said, "Jimmy, that's an awful thing to say about your grandmother!"

"But Mom," Jimmy protested, "I heard you tell Daddy that you were really 'rustrated' by how long Grandma was staying!"

With that Jimmy received a spat on his backside. "First of all, young man," the startled mother said, "you shouldn't have been eavesdropping when your Daddy and I were talking, and secondly, the word is 'frustrated', not 'rustrated.'"

Looking at his mother with surprise, feeling that her sternness somehow didn't fit as punishment for his "crime," he said, "Mom, what's frustration?"

We can laugh at the ambivalent feelings expressed by everyone in that very common relational drama. And we can feel the frustration of all concerned. But then, Jimmy's question haunts us. Not only—what is frustration, but what or who can be a source of it in our own lives?

I was thinking about that as I boarded the plane. Guess what? I had been assigned the seat next to Grandma! After she dried her tears, she struck up a conversation. Well, not really a conversation; she did all the talking halfway to Chicago. Her nonstop monologue was interrupted only long enough to bark instructions to the flight attendants.

This woman was a frustrated boss. She could have been the Chief Executive Officer of the whole airline and still not exhausted her untapped reservoir of ideas about what everyone should be doing.

During the early part of the trip, I kept what I did for a living as a guarded secret. She would have told me how to run my ministry!

My seat companion disturbed me for two reasons. First, I wasn't able to get any work done. And, second, I felt victimized by the tyranny of her incessant talking.

After she had gone on talking nonstop for over an hour, I interrupted and told her that I'd been seated next to her and Jimmy and her daughter-in-law in the waiting lounge. Then I said, "You seemed very upset when you boarded the plane. I think that's what's really on your mind. Why don't we talk about that?" The woman's bossy attitude seemed to change, and I felt that now she might be open to conversation instead of monologue.

She began to cry again. Then, sensing my genuine concern, she told me about how important her son and his family were to her; they were her life. She had few friends and her visits with them were the only bright spot in her very lonely life.

"Do you feel close to them?" I asked. No, she didn't. In fact, she felt they dreaded her visits and were glad when she left. When I asked why she thought this might be so, she responded with some self-pitying complaints that they didn't need her and no one really cared about her. With that, I took a deep breath, gathered my courage, and said, "Could it be that your actions contribute to that feeling?"

The rest of the trip to Chicago was filled with deeper exchange than I would have imagined possible. I shared with her the fact that I was a Christian and talked about how the Lord could help us with the problem of loneliness. "Only Christ can meet our deepest needs," I confided. "He can change our attitudes and help us to love rather than manipulate or control people. Perhaps you need Jimmy and his parents too much, and you need to set them free to live their own lives."

By the end of the flight, we had reached the deeper cause

of her problem: She desperately needed Christ and some friends other than her family. Before the plane landed, I asked her if I could pray for her. After I did, she looked up and said, "Thanks, nobody's ever told me how I come across or helped me think about why. I'm going to reflect on this and see what I can do about it." We exchanged addresses and she promised to write.

I've heard from her several times since. She tells me she has made an effort to be different and has implemented some of the suggestions I made. She has given up trying to run the retirement home where she lives and has reached out to people and made some new friends. The church I recommended she attend in her neighborhood welcomed her with open arms and is using her leadership talents. Most important of all, she's growing in her new faith. Her last visit to her family was very different because the Lord, not them, is becoming her security.

This woman exemplifies so many of the needy, frustrating people in all of our lives. And not only are they in our families, but we find them among our friends, among the people with whom we work, and even among the fellow Christians with whom we share the life of our churches. Feelings of frustration are common with all of us, but I believe the Lord has an answer for this problem too. He is able to help us face and overcome our frustrations. To do that He helps us understand what frustration is and how He enables us to overcome it.

When We Feel Blocked and Thwarted

Jimmy's term "rustration" may be closer to the meaning of frustration than his mother realized. Rust forms on metal from lack of use. So often we feel frustrated when we are blocked, thwarted, or hindered by situations or people. A cap is placed on our free expression of ourselves and the fulfillment of our needs.

The definition of frustration implies that idea. Frustration is being kept back from doing or achieving something. It is the stifling of our self-expression, the limitation of our self-realization. Added to that, frustration is what we feel when we confront seemingly insurmountable obstacles between us and achieving what we want. Frustration is really disappointment.

The Latin root for the word "frustrate" is *frustraro,* which means "to disappoint." *Frustra* in Latin means "in vain." That explains our feelings. We are most frustrated when we can't seem to change people or circumstances. Frustration is really a sense of powerlessness. It's a feeling of helplessness and hopelessness. We wonder if our best efforts will make any difference.

Christ's Promise for Our Frustrations

There's a very familiar verse in our New Testament that speaks powerfully to the problem of frustration: ". . . Assuredly, I say to you, if you have faith as a mustard seed, you will say to this mountain, 'Move from here to there,' and it will move; and nothing will be impossible for you" (Matt. 17:20).

The people and things that frustrate us loom up before us like immovable mountains. In Jesus' day, the word "mountain" was used synonymously for difficult, seemingly impossible problems. A teacher who could unravel complex questions or offer solutions to difficulties was called a "mountain remover." Perhaps this is what the Master had in mind when He told the disciples that even a miniscule faith could remove a mighty mountain. When we consider the context in which Jesus spoke this startling promise, its implications for us become even clearer.

A Picture of Frustration

Catch the full impact of the drama. Jesus had left ten of the disciples behind in the valley while He, Peter, and John went up on a mountain. While they were gone, the disciples experienced the frustration of human impotence. A man brought his epileptic son seeking Jesus' healing. When he realized that Jesus was not there, he asked the disciples to heal the boy. The disciples had healed people before. Jesus had given them the power of exorcism and healing when He had sent them out to preach and teach (Matt. 10). So, it was natural that the man ask the disciples to pray for the healing of his son. And yet, they were not able to heal the boy. But when Jesus returned, He healed him. Why were the disciples unable to heal in this instance? What was wrong?

Mark elaborates on this same event by telling us that a great crowd had gathered around the boy, his father, and the disciples. Most of them were probably just curious. Also we are told that there were scribes in the crowd. They were not curious, but hostile. Along with the Pharisees, they had dogged the tracks of Jesus and the disciples wherever they went, inflicting a pall of negativism. Possibly their hostile attitude had made the disciples self-conscious and defensive, blocking the flow of Jesus' healing power through them.

The Lack of Faith

Jesus' analysis of the situation was very incisive. "O faithless and perverse generation, how long shall I be with you?" Were these sharp, biting words said in anger? I don't think so. Rather, they express a frank recognition of the lack of faith in Him that was the secret of the release of His power.

In this scene we feel His urgency to get on with the reason He had come into the world. Jesus knew that the gift of faith would not come in full measure until after His Crucifixion and Resurrection. Then, through the infilling of His Spirit at Pentecost, a new faith-filled generation would be born. And, by faith in Him as Savior and Lord, His supernatural power would replace the impotence of human frustration.

Perhaps it was this anticipation that explains Jesus' response to a question the disciples asked Him in private. They wanted to know why they had not been able to cast out the demon they assumed was causing his sickness: "Why could *we* not cast him out?" (Matt. 17:19, italics mine). Note the emphasis on the pronoun "we." Had they tried to heal in their own strength? Had they forgotten Jesus' command that power would be released only in *His* name?

The Lord cut to the core of the problem in His response. "Because of your unbelief," He said pointedly. Other translations of His diagnosis read, "Because of your lack of faith." This is not a condemnatory analysis of their condition, but an honest recognition that at that point the gift of faith had not been released. Jesus was not criticizing the disciples for lack of a humanly induced confidence that they could heal an epileptic. Faith was given as a gift after the Cross and Resurrection and the infilling of His Spirit at Pentecost. Then, filled with the power of faith they claimed their forgiveness through the cross. The Resurrection became their power to live a new life. And Christ indwelling in them was the source of their daring boldness to believe that through Him all things were possible.

Faith, Power, and Prayer

Now we can understand the "if" of Jesus' tremendous qualification, "If you have faith as a mustard seed." The quantity of faith wasn't the issue—it was the quality of authentic faith He would give them. The mustard seed was so small it could hardly be seen by the naked eye. And yet, from it, a large bushy tree could grow.

There's a great truth in all this for us. For it is as we receive the faith to accept the forgiveness of the Cross and the Resurrection, and experience His presence in us, that we can confront the "mountains" of life and say, "Move from here to there!" And it will be moved. Anything the Lord wills will be possible. Jesus concluded His promise in Matthew 17:20

with a reminder that prayer will be the secret for facing our frustrations and receiving the strength we need to overcome them. Considering the promise as a whole, the Lord has offered us donated faith, a derived power, and the dynamic access of prayer. It is exciting to reflect on this promise in that order, keeping in mind the frustrating circumstances, situations, and people we are facing right now.

When Mountains and Faith Meet

William Blake said, "Great things are done when Men & Mountains meet. This is not done by Jostling in the Street."* You and I are more than jostlers in the street. I would reword Blake's line: "Great things happen when people of faith and mountains meet. For them frustration does not spell their defeat." All of us have very real frustrations that become like mountains in our way. But we are not stopped. We have a "donated faith," a gift from the Lord to trust Him to show us how to conquer those mountains. He helps us understand His plans and goals for us. His mountain-removing power is available for that, not just for removing the little irritations of life. When some frustrating person or situation stands in the way of our being obedient to Him, He gives us the power to believe that they can be moved.

Notice that the power we are given is to say to our mountains, "Move from here to there." The promise is that the mountain will be moved out of the way of our progress. The Lord did not say that through faith we would always be able to get rid of our mountains. What He did promise is that He will help us move them out of the way.

But that moving of the mountain begins inside us. Often our attitude toward the mountain is more debilitating than the mountain itself. We become defensive, allowing the people

---

* *The Poetry and Prose of William Blake,* ed. David V. Erdman (Garden City, NY: Doubleday, 1965), p. 502.

or problems that are our mountains to make us think they are controlling our destiny.

I am convinced that Jesus is talking about our discipleship in this metaphor of the mountain. When we commit our lives to Him, following Him obediently becomes the issue. Along the way, frustrating mountains do loom before us. But that's when He gives us the faith to say, "Be removed from here to there. I'm going to obey my Lord and press on to His goals for me!"

The transfer of the mountain from an obstructing position to one side is the beginning part of the miracle the Lord performs. It happens first in our minds in our perception of the mountain. The Lord must first convince us that nothing or no one can stand in our way in moving forward in His purposes for us. And, when that's accomplished, we can confront the mountains in His name and with His power.

Prayer and Our Frustrations

The dynamic access to the presence of the Lord in prayer is how we use our donated faith and derived power. When a frustration threatens to stand in the way of our commitment to Christ, we need to allow the Lord to condition our minds. He gives us wisdom to see whether the mountain is simply an irritation or a real obstruction. Then He helps us to understand the real nature of the mountain—why are the people who frustrate us acting the way they do? Why do they upset us? The same gift of insight is given us about circumstances. What is the real problem presented to us in the circumstances? What does the Lord will for us in them? How does He want us to react? What does He want us to do?

It's when we have that quality of openness that faith is released. We are given the vision of what life would be like without the mountain in our way. Then we can pray that the vision will come true. And in answer, power is released in us to replace the tension of trying to handle the frustration ourselves. At the same time, the Lord is working in the person or situation that is frustrating us. He changes attitudes and resolves what seemed to be impossible complications. It is then that we can be assured of His impossibility-dispelling power to work for us to set the mountains aside, out of the way of our path of faithfulness to Him.

Now, let's be very practical in illustrating how this happens in the real life frustrations that disturb us.

Physical Frustrations

Some of us are frustrated by illness or disabilities that we feel limit our happiness and our dreams for a worry-free, full life. At such times we often do more complaining to the Lord than confessing of our need for Him. My experience of praying for healing is that the Lord seldom removes the mountains of our illness until it has been used to drive us back to complete trust in Him. Only when we want Him and a profound relationship with Him more than anything else can we experience the full meaning and power of His healing.

That deeper healing happened in the life of a friend of mine. I had been praying for him for a long time. He believed in the Lord's power to heal his serious illness. Often, he came forward at the close of our worship services for prayer with the pastors and elders. There was little change in his condition. Meanwhile, the man became increasingly frustrated by the limitation his illness placed on his ability to carry on his busy life. And, quite understandably, he was distressed that the Lord didn't seem to hear and answer his and our prayers for healing.

Then, one Sunday, he came forward with a very different kind of prayer request. He said, "I've been going about this in the wrong way. Just this morning I realized that I'd been putting the healing of my illness as a qualification for really following the Lord in my life. I realized that I wanted healing more than I wanted Him. Now I want to pray that I will put my relationship with the Lord first in my life. Whether I'm healed according to my specifications or not is no longer the issue."

That's a courageous prayer request. The mountainous frustration of his illness no longer stood in the way. At that point his illness was not taken away, but his demand that the Lord heal him before he would follow Him was removed as an obstruction on his path to the Lord Himself. Now he was the Lord's man whether he lived or died. The mountain that had stood in his way had been moved out of his path. And the heartening thing is that getting the mountain off his path in his relationship with the Lord, resulted in a radical change in his illness. In this case, the Lord healed the illness and he is alive today. But first he had to discover that the healing was for the purpose of freeing him to serve the Lord more completely.

The Real Miracle

My friend's healing sounds like a contemporary miracle. It is. But his experience is no more a miracle than a woman I know whose mountain of frustration over her illness was removed, but in her case she was not healed physically. This particular lady went through a similar process of being freed from frustration as the man I just described but she is still disabled by a crippling paralysis of part of her body. And yet, she is determined not to allow any kind of a mountain to stand in the way of being a joyful and radiant Christian. In fact, her attitude of trust and joy has been used by the Lord to witness to hundreds of other people with handicaps. She says, "I decided not to spend the rest of my life with 'what-might-have-beens.' This physical difficulty is not going to keep me from the Lord. I've given Him my feelings of frustration, and He removed them. If He chooses to remove my handicap, I'll praise Him. If He doesn't I'll still praise Him. In the meantime, there's lots of people worse off than

I who need His love and care. And they know I'm not kidding when I tell them about His love in and through difficulties."

Both of my friends had the mountain of frustration moved out of their way even though the Lord dealt differently with each of them. Both of them experienced the liberation from frustration in their minds and in their circumstances and both are on the move for the Lord as a result.

Frustrations in Relationships

A similar thing happened to a man who was frustrated by lack of deep communication in his marriage. His wife did things constantly that annoyed him. Soon she became the moving target of his endless criticism and that only made her even less open and less affectionate. Rather than accepting the idea that he might be part of the difficulty, he thought of his wife as the problem he would have to endure for the rest of his life.

One day in conversation, my frustrated friend spoke of his wife as the "cross I have to bear." I challenged that attitude and reminded him that obedience to Christ was his cross. I then asked what that obedience might mean for his attitude and actions in his marriage. He had never thought of it that way.

As we talked, it came out that he imagined that his wife and their troubled marriage were standing in his way to being a Christian. We then talked about the need for him to experience a deeper relationship with the Lord regardless of whether his marriage ever changed. I pointed out that the things she was doing were because she was a person with deep needs and only a combination of the Lord's invasion of her heart and a change in his attitude would bring about any improvement in their marriage.

We met regularly after that to talk and to pray about his marriage. Our first step was to discuss priorities. Up to this point he was depending on his marriage as the security and meaning of his life. He had allowed his frustration over not having his needs met in his marriage to keep him from prayer and fellowship with the Lord. We prayed together specifically about that, asking the Lord to remove the self-imposed mountain that he had set between himself and the growth of his faith. I pointed out that he had to be willing to say, "I'm going on with the Lord whatever happens in my marriage."

Then as a second step, we turned our attention to some radical surgery of his attitudes, actions, and responses to his wife. And then we moved on to take a close look at those things which his wife did or did not do that frustrated him. As all of this was talked out, he began to see his wife as a person in need of the Lord's love and not just as a road-block to the fulfillment of his needs. And after taking this giant step he was ready to consider what he needed to *be* and *do* in order to show his love whether she changed or not.

With this whole process of mountain removal he changed drastically in his actions and attitudes toward his wife. Out of the resources of the man's newfound intimacy with the Lord, he had so much more to give her. Being free of needing her so desperately, he was much more relaxed and fun to live with. It was at this point that his wife began to take more seriously his commitment to Christ. When she discovered she could not dissuade him from that, she became open to getting help for herself. It came out that all along she had thought her husband was her main problem, but now she began to see that her deeper problem was inside herself. She began to understand that her need was for the kind of life-changing experience her husband had. Throughout this process her husband was praying for her and showing affirmation and love for her. And it wasn't long before a miracle of grace occurred when she invited Christ to be the Lord of her life. Now they could move ahead to a marvelous new experience of love in their life together.

The startling thing about this story is that both the husband and wife were church members and considered themselves to be good Christians. But they both had been blocked by mountains of frustration that stood in their way of a right relationship with each other and the Lord. Now, those mountains were not just moved by His grace—they were removed entirely.

Frustrations at Work

I have another friend who complained about his frustrations at work. He confessed that he could not live out his faith because of the pressures of his job and the lack of appreciation from his fellow-workers and superiors. Here again was a person who allowed circumstances to keep him from the source of strength in the Lord to be faithful in those difficult circumstances. That was his real mountain. He feared losing his job and the comfortable living it allowed him to provide for his family. Unfortunately he had never stopped to think that possibly the Lord had placed him in those difficult circumstances in order for him to live out and share his faith. He was too panicked about success for that.

Another member of my church who had gone through a similar problem saw the telltale signs of the man's stress. He befriended him and eventually won the right to help the man surrender his mountain and make a commitment of his future to the Lord.

As time went on, these two men met regularly and soon other business people who faced similar problems joined them. Now they meet weekly to discuss how they can be the Lord's people in their work situations. Their mountains of fear have been removed as they discovered that the real obstruction was in their minds. They pray for each other for daily problems that loom up. Previously, these problems would have been thought of as impossible mountains in their paths. They are an adventuresome band of mountain-removers by the power of the Lord.

Dealing with Frustrating People

Probably nothing is more frustrating in our Christian pilgrimage than people, but even they do not need to keep us from our commitment to the Lord. In fact, only the Lord can help us cope with them. We do not need to be victims of difficult people! We choose to be victimized. And it is our lack of strength in the Lord that often leaves us vulnerable to being manipulated. The Lord wants us to be free from any bondage to frustrating and troublesome people. Then, as free people, we can lovingly, but firmly, share what I like to call the "irreducible maximum" of our values, direction, and desires for our lives as Christians. And, in an atmosphere of love and caring, we can talk out the things that frustrate us in the difficult people of our lives.

Does that always work? No, but it does much of the time. Once the mountain is out of the way in our minds and we are in the flow of the Lord's grace, we can share what is distressing us. That attitude on our part often helps the other person to unload the reason he or she has been acting in a frustrating way. At the same time we may learn that we've been frustrating them too!

Of course, there are times we have to "shake the dust off our feet" and move on in following the Master. Not all relationships with frustrating people can be solved. We must remember that people have the free will not to change. But they should not keep us from the ones who can and will change.

But, by far the most important thing for our relationship with the Lord and for peace of mind is that we commit to Him whatever or whomever is the "mountain" we perceive is standing in our way. Remember He can change us and our attitude. And after the removal of that high-reaching mountain—whatever it is—nothing that He wills is impossible. We can be free of frustration!

8

THE ONLY SURE CURE FOR AN ANXIOUS MIND

"IF I KNOW GOD CARES, why do I still react to problems with anxiety? If God is in charge, why do I expend vital energy being anxious over His timing and strategy in solving problems?" In other words, "Why are we so anxious so much of the time?"

Hundreds of people responded to my survey about problems by asking questions like these.

These recent years are often referred to as "the age of anxiety," and for good reason. It is this epidemic of anxiety that we will turn our attention to now.

The Problem of Anxious Thinking

Most of us suffer from what I call anxious thinking. And since feelings follow thought, feelings of anxiety are triggered by anxious thinking. This simply means that as anxious

thinking becomes habitual, we are constantly upset emotionally. Eventually, the feelings of anxiety begin to dominate
our thinking and we become "irrational" in our responses
to life—anxious without any apparent cause.

How can we stop having an anxious mind? Hardly an hour
passes in any day without the debilitating toll of anxious thinking invading our thought processes and filling our emotions
with distress and our bodies with stress agitation. And, so
we ask again, how is it possible to keep from thinking anxiously?

Wishing and Hoping

One of the most effective ways to avoid this kind of negative
thinking is to stop wishing and start hoping. There's a great
difference between wishing and hoping. Wishing is a longing
desire for some thing or some happening. It is rooted in what
we want—something we think will bring us happiness, success,
or fulfillment. We want some desire to be fulfilled, some plan
to be accomplished, or some problem to be worked out to
our advantage. Wishing is humanly induced.

On the other hand, hoping, for the Christian, is much more
profound. Its roots are planted deeply in the promises of the
Lord and in prayer for His guidance. Hope has force behind
it because it is the focus of what He has led us to envision
and expect. It also has confidence and peace because it trusts
completely the timing and pacing of the Lord's plans for us.
Hoping arises out of prolonged, intimate prayerful communion
with the Lord in which we open ourselves completely to Him.
The Christian's hope is the result of the question, "Lord, what
do You want me to do, to dare to attempt, to be in these
challenges and opportunities before me? What is Your strategy?
What will produce Your ultimate good for me and all the
people involved? Guide my thinking and remold my thoughts

around Your maximum purpose for me. Show me Your long-range plans for me and Your short-range goals for my immediate problems, so I can move ahead toward Your vision for my life." It is out of that kind of disciplined prayer-thought, that clearly defined hopes are formed. Then we can face life with the confidence that what the Lord guides us to hope for, He provides.

The opposite of that kind of hope is willful wishing. It's what pops into our minds before we have checked it out with the Lord. The tentacles of that kind of wishing are attached to deeper desires which may not have been transformed by Him. Pride, self-centeredness, selfishness, envy, jealousy, and the will to control can be the feeding ground of some of our most ardent wishes. The wish itself may appear magnanimous on the surface but the motivation behind it may be less than creative for us or people involved.

But by far the most frustrating part of wishful thinking is that we must pull it off by our own effort, striving, and manipulation. Because these kinds of wishes have not been conditioned by prayer, we are left to our own resources to accomplish them. Often after these wishes are firmly set we ask the Lord to bless them. And we end up telling Him what's best, what we want Him to do so things will work out in line with our wishes. That's why many Christians are anxious even after making a confession of belief in Christ and in attempting to live the Christian life. Their lives are still under their own management and they have no strength other than their own to accomplish their wish-dreams.

All of us find it easy to slip into living by our wishes rather than by Spirit-guided hopes. Because we are unsure of what the Lord wants of us, we are also uncertain as to whether we can depend on His power to accomplish what we want. Even as Christians, we may live for days, months, even a lifetime, on the level of wishing. Often, it takes a really big problem to alarm us of the kind of anxious thinking which has become the habit of our minds.

Jesus' Promise for Overcoming Anxious Thinking

What does Jesus have to say about this? Has He given us a promise as a sure cure for this kind of anxious thinking? Yes. He gives us a prohibition with a promise followed by an admonition and an assurance. "And do not seek what you should eat or what you should drink, *nor have an anxious mind.* For all these things the nations of the world seek after, and your Father knows that you need these things. But seek the kingdom of God, and all these things shall be added to you. Do not fear, little flock, for it is your Father's good pleasure to give you the kingdom" (Luke 12:29–32, italics mine).

We mustn't allow the familiarity of these words to blunt our minds from cutting into the profound meaning of Jesus' prescription for anxious thinking.

Note the development of the Master's thought in these four verses from Luke. First, He says, "Don't have an anxious mind." Why? Because the Father knows your needs. Then He tells us to seek the kingdom of God. Why? Because it is the Father's good pleasure to give it to you—He is the source of the desire to discover His guidance as the basis of our hoping. Let's allow Jesus' progression of thought to guide us in understanding and living His answer to the problem of anxious thinking.

Meteoric Thinking

Let's look first at the prohibition and the promise. A careful look at the Greek adjective Luke selected to record Jesus' Aramaic word for *anxious* is very revealing and exciting. Luke was a thoughtful scholar, schooled and fluent in Greek. He used a different word than is found in the Greek text of Matthew's recording of the same statement (Matt. 6:31). It is not *merimnēsēte,* from *merimnaō,* as used by Matthew, but *meteōrizesthe,* from *meteōrizō.*

The Greek word *merimnaō*, meaning "to care," "to have a worrisome thought," is the word used by Matthew throughout his recording of the section of the Sermon on the Mount dealing with anxiety. Luke uses this same word in 12:26: "If you then are not able to do the least, why are you anxious for the rest?" But then in verse 29 Luke uses a different word for "anxious," a word not used elsewhere in Luke's Gospel or in the entire New Testament. He used this word because it expressed precisely what Jesus really meant when He said, "And do not have an anxious mind." It stands out like an exclamation point.

The basic verb from which the adjective Luke uses comes from *meteōros*, meaning "high in the air." *Meteōron* is a thing high in the air—*meta-*, "beyond," *eōra-*, "suspension." We can easily identify the close relationship between this Greek word and our word "meteor." And we know that a meteor is a small mass of matter which, when it strikes the earth's atmosphere with great velocity, explodes and burns out. This is most descriptive of so much of our wishful thinking—like a meteor, brilliant in its flight, but dissipated when it collides with reality.

Building on that idea, we need to consider the development of this interesting word *meteōros* in the Greek world of Luke's experience. By degrees, it had come to describe a person who was lifted up with wishes, wild thinking, or vain imaginings. As an adjective descriptive of a type of thinking, *meteōrizesthe*, it depicted elevated desires unfounded in realism, thoughts shot up like meteors which are quickly dissipated. It is to be buoyed up with self-aggrandizing, but false longings.

All of this deepens our appreciaton of why Luke, under the guidance of the Holy Spirit, employed *meteōrizesthe* to express Jesus' meaning when He cautioned against anxious thinking. Our Lord was exposing lofty wishes which became set in goals. Then when they are not fulfilled according to our time schedule and in a way pleasing to us, we become disappointed and worried. In short, *meteōrizesthe*, anxious thinking, is using the ability of imagination and vision to generate our own wish-dreams and then stewing over how, if, and when *we* can make them come true.

We all know about that kind of thinking and what it does to us. "Wishing upon a star" can be very discouraging when the star is nothing more than our own self-projected meteor. We have seen too many such meteors stream across the sky of our experience and then burn out. So many of the wishes we've had for ourselves, loved ones, friends, our careers, and situations have sputtered into oblivion. Add to that the longings of what we have desired to possess for our own comfort or status, and it's no wonder we become anxious. Attempting to be, do, or have what has not been clearly guided by the Lord floods the mind with anxious thoughts and with feelings of uneasy insecurity. But feeling the pain of insecurity makes us ready for Jesus' solution.

We are told in these words of Jesus not to continue to send up our meteorlike wish-dreams because God knows what we need. He is thinking about us! He created us with ability to think so that He could think His thoughts through us. That's what dynamic prayer is—thinking God's thoughts after Him.

And He's always ready to guide our thinking. He is omniscient, all-knowing. That is both encouraging and comforting. He knows our thoughts, wishes, and plans and is constantly impinging on our thought processes seeking to inspire us with His guidance. He created us and knows the power of thought to shape our destiny. And because He loves us, He wants to transform thoughts which will eventually cause us anxiety.

The First Step

The first step to overcoming anxious thinking then is to make an unreserved commitment of our minds to the Lord, asking Him to guide and direct our thinking so that our thoughts can be conformed to His will for us. Paul encouraged the Philippians, "Let this mind be in you which was also in

Christ Jesus" (Phil. 2:5). So often we think of the ministry of the indwelling Christ in us only as a source of strength and courage. But He offers us so much more. He captures our thinking and guides the development of our hopes.

From within our minds, the Lord expands our thinking to include possibilities our self-generated wishing would never have dared envision. He gives us a picture of what He will do in and around us. No need to be anxious about the accomplishment of these hopes. They are backed up by the promises and power of the Lord Himself.

The Second Step

The second step is a basic formula to use in the development of our hopes. It is contained in the admonition and assurance Jesus gives after telling us not to have an anxious mind and giving us the promise that God knows. "But seek the kingdom of God, and all these things shall be added to you. Do not fear, little flock, for it is your Father's good pleasure to give you the kingdom" (Luke 12:31–32). Note the close connection between "Seek the kingdom of God" and "it is your Father's good pleasure to give you the kingdom."

The kingdom of God is His rule and reign in us, in our relationships, and in all the affairs of life. When the Lord's will is our dominate desire, He will use many different ways to make it abundantly clear. The Bible, prayer, meditation, circumstances, insights from trusted fellow Christians—will all be utilized to guide us. Our part is to commit our minds to kingdom thinking and hoping rather than meteoric wishing and yearning.

The Kingdom of Our Minds

A woman by the name of Thelma has discovered this secret of overcoming anxious thinking. She told me that for years after she became a Christian she remained a "troubled, fretting, anxious person." Her strong will kept her in a bind. "I'd think through what was best for me, my family, our church, and all my friends, and then spend hours telling the Lord what I wanted. Often I would get impatient and step in to be sure things worked out as I had decided was best. Usually I made a mess of things and was constantly worried. 'Why didn't God do something?' I'd wonder. Then I'd feel a combination of anger and disappointment. I believed and prayed, but still I was anxious."

One day while visiting over a cup of coffee we talked through her dilemma. I felt led to ask, "Thelma, what do you consider to be the most important gift you have to offer the Lord in guiding your life?" After a long pause she said, "Why of course, my thinking brain." That gave me an opening. "Have you ever thought about the kingdom of your mind?" I questioned further. "When you committed your life to Christ, did you specifically include your thinking? Remember all of our values, goals, purposes, self-image, and attitudes are stored there. Did you ask the Lord to reform your mind to be like His? Did you ask Him to take charge of your thinking about the future? The vital throne of the King of the kingdom is in your brain. If He doesn't reign supreme there, it will be difficult to make Him King over your relationships and circumstances."

A very important change took place in Thelma that day. She made a new commitment to Christ, surrendering her thinking and decisions to Him. An aspect of that commitment resulted in a greater amount of time spent in prayer. She now takes half an hour at the beginning of every day to be quiet. After reading a passage in the Bible, she prayerfully reviews all the problems and challenges before her. Most of the rest of her prayer time is spent asking for the Lord to clarify, shape, and solidify her thinking. She is amazed at how often her thinking and plans are changed and her limited expectations are expanded to include possibilities she never would have imagined on her own.

But the most significant result is in her new freedom from anxiety about life and people. She now lives by hope in the Lord's faithfulness rather than by wishes she must try to accomplish with her own determination and effort. Over the months, the Lord has transformed Thelma's thinking.

Resisting Guidance

But what about the times when we resist and block the Lord's guidance of our thoughts? We are reminded that some of our biblical heroes had as difficult a time as we sometimes do yielding the kingdom of their minds.

Look at Peter at the time he was challenged to extend the gospel to the Gentile world. In Acts 10 we are shown the process the Lord used to change his thinking. Up to this point Peter's mind was dominated with the idea that Christ was the Messiah of the Hebrew people. His thinking was limited by exclusivism and he had not comprehended that Christ's commission to go and make disciples of all nations included the Gentiles.

One day at noon Peter was praying on a rooftop of a house in Joppa. He had a shocking vision of a sheet being let down from heaven containing animals and beasts which were forbidden and declared unfit by Hebrew food laws. Then, Peter heard a voice saying "Rise, Peter; kill and eat." Peter's vehement response was, "Not so, Lord!" The vision and the command were repeated three times, and we suspect, so was Peter's objection. Then he began to wonder what the vision meant. The Lord was driving a wedge in his exclusive thinking. He was soon to learn that it was not his food laws that were the issue but a Gentile the Lord had been preparing to receive the gospel.

The day before the Lord had interrupted the prayers of Cornelius, a devout centurion in Caesarea. The Roman had been profoundly influenced by the Hebrew religion. In a vision he was told to send his servants to Joppa to find Peter and bring him to Caesarea.

The messengers arrived for Peter while he was still trying to sort out what the Lord was trying to tell him in his strange vision on the rooftop. The Spirit told Peter not to doubt but to receive them. The apostle followed orders and invited the Gentile messengers to spend the night. That in itself was remarkable for the strict Hebrew. I think it was when Peter was told by the messengers that Cornelius had been divinely instructed to summon him that he began to wonder about the relationship of his vision and the one given to Cornelius. What was the Lord trying to tell him? He probably thought and prayed about that all night and the next day on his journey to Caesarea.

Somewhere in the process the Lord radically changed Peter's thinking. It is evident by the time he reached Cornelius's house he had put together his vision and the call from Cornelius. When the apostle entered the centurion's house he said, "You know how unlawful it is for a Jewish man to keep company with or go to one of another nation. But God has shown me that I should not call any man common or unclean" (Acts 10:28). The vision had worked!

The Lord had changed Peter's thinking. His "Not so!" became an obedient "Yes, Lord." The result was that he preached the gospel to Cornelius and his whole household. While he was preaching the Spirit was poured out upon them all. A new Pentecost happened in a Gentile centurion's home in Caesarea. Peter was never the same after that. Nor was the early church. The conversion of Cornelius became crucial in the Lord's breaking open Peter's thinking to include the Gentile world in his vision for the expansion of the church.

We all can think of times we've balked at some guidance from the Lord and said, "Not so, Lord!" Perhaps we're in some wrestling match right now in which we are thinking it. There will be anxiety and no peace until we cross off the

"Not so" and simply say "Lord!" in awe and wonder at what
He desires to do through us. He's always out ahead of us
arranging new possibilities.

The Lord's "Yes Man"

In my relationships the last thing I'd ever want to be called
is a "yes man." But in my relationship with the Lord that's
exactly what I long to be more consistently—the Lord's "yes
man"! And when I am, I can say "yes" to what He guides
and be free to say "no" to anything which leads me away
from His maximum strategy for me.

G. Campbell Morgan expressed how this kind of guided
thinking brings freedom from anxiety. "The supreme passion
of all our days, in all our ways, is to be a person for the
kingdom of God. That is not some far off reality or event,
but something already existing, in which and with which we
are to seek right relationships. The passion of life is to be a
passion for the kingdom of God, and the measure to which
we obey this injunction (to seek first the kingdom), is the
measure in which we pass into the realm of unruffled peace
and rest and calm."

A Helpful Inventory

Sometimes it's helpful for me to pause and reflect on some
challenging thought I've discovered. I feel the need to do
that about what we've discussed in this chapter. You may
want to do the same.

What makes us anxious right now? Let's try to trace the
feelings back to our thinking about the people or situations
involved. What meteor-wishes are you straining to pull off?
Have we taken the time to prayerfully discover the Lord's
guidance as the basis of hoping and not just wishing?

I don't know about you, but asking those questions has
focused relationships and responsibilities in which I need to
listen more intently to the Lord's guidance.

When I get caught in the syndrome of anxious thinking about an area of my life I try to remember Hudson Taylor's words about pressure. It applies equally well for problems. "It doesn't matter, really" said the missionary leader of the China Inland Mission, "how great the pressure is; it only matters where the pressure lies. See that it never comes between you and the Lord—then, the greater the pressure the more it presses you to Him." That leads me to ask myself, and you: Is the pressure of life behind us pressing us to the Lord because we have surrendered it to His guiding thought control? Or is it dividing us from Him?

I like J. N. Darley's translation of the Hebrew of Psalm 4:1, "When I call, answer me, O God my righteousness: in pressure Thou hast enlarged me; be gracious unto me, and hear my prayer." That's one prayer the Lord is sure to answer. He motivates us to pray it so He can also answer it and replace our wishes with hope rooted in His clear direction. Then we can join the company of heaven with our anxiety-dispelling "Alleluia, for the Lord God Omnipotent reigns" (Rev. 19:6).

And so we ask again the question with which we opened this chapter. "If God cares, *why am I* anxious about problems?" Why indeed!

"I believe"—but, do I? Am I sure?
Can I trust my trusting to endure?
Can I hope that my belief will last?
Will my hand forever hold Him fast?
Am I certain I am saved from sin?
Do I feel His presence here within?
Do I hear Him tell me that He cares?
Do I see the answers to my prayers?
Do no fears my confidence assail?
Do I know my faith will never fail?

"I believe"—ay, do I! I believe
He will never fail me, never leave;
I believe He holds me, and I know
His strong hand will never let me go;

Seeing, hearing, feeling—what are these?
Given or withheld as He shall please.
I believe in Him and what He saith;
I have faith in Him, not in my faith
That may fail, tomorrow or today;
Trust may weaken, feeling pass away,
Thoughts grow weary, anxious, or depressed;
I believe in God—and here I rest.

Annie Johnson Flint

9

TOO SOON OLD, TOO LATE FREE

LAST THANKSGIVING DAY, I had a very moving experience of rediscovering the child in me. During a service of praise at my church, I asked all the children present to come and sit with me on the chancel steps for a children's sermon.

I was delighted when they came surging forward and sat around me. One young boy scampered up on my lap, a little girl cuddled up beside me, and the rest gathered around me with enthusiasm. It was great fun to look into the shining faces of children, their eyes sparkling with excitement.

I started my little sermon by asking the children to tell me what they were thankful for. And believe me, they were not shy about responding—pets, family, friends, and even their Thanksgiving turkeys roasting in the ovens at home.

One little girl, Ginger, kept waving her arm, asking for a chance to express what she was thankful for. She would not be put off. I could see there wasn't any possibility of going on until she had her say. So, I leaned over and held the microphone up to her ear-to-ear grin.

"Dr. Ogilvie," Ginger said naturally and warmly, "I'm thankful for you!"

The congregation laughed and then clapped in appreciation for the little girl's willingness to express herself so freely. She thought they were laughing at her and that she had done something wrong. So I gave her a big hug, assured her she had said a wonderful thing, and thanked her for her special gift of love to me. Then I added, "I'm thankful for you, too."

The children picked up the cue and spontaneously turned and told the other children around them that they were thankful for them. There was no giggling or embarrassment—just the fun of a happy exchange in the spirit of thanksgiving.

What was happening to the children was contagious. Soon the members of the choir followed their lead and turned to each other expressing their gratitude. Several got up out of their seats and expressed appreciation to the choir director and then the organist. The pastors followed suit, and quickly the whole congregation was buzzing with "I'm thankful for you!" as people shook hands, hugged, and expressed love to others around them. It was a great moment of unfettered Thanksgiving joy. I felt warm all over as I allowed the child inside me to laugh and burst out with gratitude for my congregation. How wonderful! It was the children who led the way into this marvelous experience.

How quickly we lose the spontaneity we had as children. As we grow older, our enthusiasm is replaced by caution, freedom is lost to self-consciousness, and trust is exchanged for a calculating evaluation of people.

Too Soon Old, Too Late Smart?

During the time I lived in Bethlehem, Pennsylvania, I really enjoyed studying the habits and culture of the Pennsylvania Dutch. Their pithy sayings were of particular interest. One of them has stuck in my mind ever since: "Too soon old, too late smart." Not a bad analysis of life, is it?

Life does slip by quickly, and often too late do we become "smart" about its ways and relationships. But that depends on what we mean by smart. Do we mean being worldly wise? . . . Wary of certain kinds of people? . . . Cautious about the dangers, pitfalls, and difficulties of living?

Perhaps we need to restate the saying, "Too soon smart, too soon old." Often our smartness makes us inhibited, fearful, and reserved. The process of growing up forces us to lose the spontaneity of childlike enthusiasm. So often life seems to be filled with potential harm from disturbed people and frightening situations. Helping a child grow into his or her teens and on to adulthood with "street-caution" and "people-smarts" without filling them with dread and panic about life is a formidable challenge, especially in our cities today.

Too Soon Old, Too Late Free

But an even greater difficulty for us who are adults is *not* losing the child in us. And so I want to reword the old Pennsylvania Dutch saying still further, "Too soon old, too late free."

So many of us are old before our time. In fact, I have come to believe that "oldness" is not a matter of age at all. It's a condition of mind. I know some young adults who have geriatric attitudes while still in their middle twenties. And, I know people in their forties who have stopped enjoying life and are not growing intellectually or spiritually. Some of my friends who are in their fifties act grim and gray. On the other hand, I know some chronologically older people who have a youthful vibrancy about them. They may be in the winter season by age, but they have never lost the spring of enthusiasm in their hearts.

My mail often brings me some interesting insights. One woman asked, "Is it possible to take life seriously without losing our spontaneity?" A letter from a man read, "How quickly I lost the enthusiasm and delight I had as a young man. Life has its burdens and I want to be responsible to carry my share of the load. Sometimes I get bogged down. I just turned forty and my wife tells me I'm acting like I'm seventy. That disturbs me. I guess I'm in a rut. What can I do to make the next forty years more of an adventure and less of a drudgery?"

Another man expressed it this way, "I hear a lot about Christians being free. I've been a member of a church for some time now. And yet, I don't feel free nor do I know many Christians who are free. I think we are as bound up as people who make no profession of believing in Christ. Exactly what does it mean to be free in Christ? I seem to have missed something!"

All of these statements express the "too soon old, too late free" problem that is common to most of us in varying degrees. Life does have its burdens and people do disappoint us. We become guarded and lose our spontaneous enthusiasm about life. Many can honestly say with Robert Louis Stevenson—

> Sing me a song of a lad that is gone,
> Say, could that lad be I?
> Give me again all that was there,
> Give me the sun that shone!
> Give me the eyes, give me the soul
> Give me the lad that's gone!*

A few weeks ago, after a graveside service for a friend of mine, I had a few moments of quiet to walk around and observe the epitaphs on the various gravestones. It made me wonder what I would want to have my family put on mine someday. Have you ever thought about that? What kind of a statement would summarize your life? Here's what I came up with. "He lived life to the fullest—spontaneously, one day at a time."

True Greatness

If we are to live life to the fullest—spontaneously, one day at a time, we must claim Christ's promise of greatness. The

---

* "My Wife," *The Collected Poems of Robert Louis Stevenson,* ed. J. Adam Smith (London: 1950).

secret of spontaneous—free, unguarded living—is found in Matthew 18:4: "Therefore whoever humbles himself as this little child is the greatest in the kingdom of heaven." To fully appreciate what that promise means, it will be helpful to focus on the scene in which the Master spoke it, but with a present tense perspective.

Jesus is seated, teaching a great crowd of people at Capernaum. They're listening intently, spellbound by the impelling power of His words. Suddenly, we're surprised by a little boy who presses his way through the crowd, eluding the grasp of those who try to catch him and pull him back. As he makes it to the inner circle of the crowd, the Master smiles at him warmly. It's obvious by the boy's response that they are friends. Those who want to push him aside realize that Jesus is pleased that the boy has come to listen and make no further effort to send him away. We are impressed with the boy's attentiveness and openness to Jesus. Love and admiration sparkle in his youthful eyes, as Jesus continues to speak. And it is obvious that Jesus is appreciative of the boy's apparent enthusiasm.

Suddenly, Jesus' disciples brusquely push open a corridor in the tightly compacted crowd and obtrusively elbow their way to the Master. When they finally reach Jesus, they interrupt His teaching with an impertinent question, "Who then is greatest in the kingdom of heaven?" From their manner, it seems likely they had been arguing this question among themselves.

We look at Jesus, wondering what His response will be. He doesn't seem to be either ruffled or surprised by the interruption or the demanding tone in the disciples' voices. Not long before, He had told them about the kingdom of heaven He had come to establish. But they had missed the point. They were thinking of a political kingdom with Him as King. Now they wanted to know who among them would be greatest, given the most recognition, authority, and power in that kingdom.

Jesus does not answer their imperious question immediately.

Instead, He looks at the young boy standing nearby and motions him to come forward. The boy responds with enthusiasm, running to Him and climbing up on His lap. The Master puts His arm around the boy and then turns to speak to the disciples. "Assuredly, I say to you, unless you are converted and become as little children, you will by no means enter the kingdom of heaven. Therefore, whoever humbles himself as this little child is the greatest in the kingdom of heaven" (Matt. 18:3–4).

What an amazing response! To those squabbling, competitive disciples jockeying for position, Jesus said in effect, "You are arguing over who is greatest in the kingdom? You haven't even entered the kingdom yet! To do that you must be converted and express the humility of a child, like this boy."

The disciples are stunned by the forthrightness of the Master. Taken back, they have nothing further to say. They are annoyed with themselves and each other for posing such a question. Then, looking at the boy on Jesus' lap, they see his complete trust and sheer joy of just being with the Master. And it begins to dawn on them what's missing in their relationship with Him.

And, as we picture that scene, it begins to dawn on us also. Jesus has defined greatness in a very startling way. What was it that He saw in that little boy that made him a model for us?

I believe this little boy modeled three important traits—the delight of life, the desire for life, and a dependence on Jesus to find that life. All three are part of His promise that we need to claim in order to overcome our "too soon old, too late free" problem.

The Delight of Life

First, Jesus affirmed the delight of life. That's what He liked so much about this little boy. The key word He used to describe this quality is humility.

What does being delighted with life have to do with

humility? Everything! The Greek meaning of the word "humility" denotes adaptability, moldability, flexibility, receptivity. A humble person is open to learn and to grow. Life is not blighted yet with the false sophistication of pretending that we know everything and have arrived. The rigors of resistance to the new, different, and untried have not set in. Life is still an exciting adventure.

For me, spontaneity is the essence of humility. Spontaneity is freedom to respond to life, to react to the opportunity of the moment. Spontaneity is to live in the now and be constantly surprised by what the Lord is able to do with our problems.

In Hebrew, an aspect of the meaning of the word "humility" is attentiveness. That's implied in Micah's use of the word, "He has shown you, O man, what is good; and what does the Lord require of you but to do justly, to love mercy, and to walk humbly with your God?" (Mic. 6:8). To walk humbly with God is to live in fellowship with Him.

The prophet Amos asks a pointed question about walking humbly with God, "Can two walk together, unless they are agreed?" (Amos 3:3). Of course not. For two people to walk together humbly, attentively listening to what each other is saying, they must go in the same direction, at the same pace, in close proximity, and toward the same destination. You can't carry on a conversation while walking unless all these elements are combined. A humble walk with God is one in which we delight in the privilege of communion with Him and are completely open to what He has to say.

When we combine the meaning of "humble" from both the Greek and the Hebrew, we can understand why Jesus affirmed humility as one of the great virtues of a child. Children are unashamedly aware of their needs. They know that they don't know everything and are open to learn. It is only when we assume the false pretenses of being an adult that we try to cover our lack of knowledge.

The little boy's humble, pliable mind presented a vivid contrast to so many of the people in the crowd that day. We are sure the scribes and Pharisees were there with their closed minds and self-satisfied attitudes. And the disciples' arrogance expressed in their dispute over who was greatest in the kingdom, displayed their unwillingness to hear what Jesus had been telling them all through His ministry with them. They were all wrapped up in what they wanted from Jesus rather than open to what He wanted to give them.

John Ruskin was right about that kind of self-interest: "When a man is all wrapped up in himself, he makes a pretty small package." Jesus wants to unwrap that package of bound-up potential before it's too late. "The only difference between a rut and a grave," said Ellen Glascow, "is the dimensions." Not so. The ruts of sameness need not be as permanent as the grave. Admitting that we're in one is the first leg up out of the rut!

Here are some questions I ask myself to test if I have the childlike delight in learning and living that Jesus stresses as so important. Am I growing, intellectually and spiritually? Am I more excited about what is ahead than what I've learned or experienced in the past? Am I enthused about the sheer wonder of being alive? Am I spontaneous in my response to each new challenge as an opportunity to discover something I've never known before?

Well, how'd you do? Is the childlike spirit of adventure still alive in you?

I like the way Helen Hayes expressed the child in her. "I'm having the best time, now! So late? You wonder. The advantage of being at this point in my life is that I neither look back nor forward—more than a few days at a time. I just enjoy now."* Her enthusiasm forces us to think about all the past memories and furtive worries about the future which rob us of living on tip-toe in the present.

Two years ago, I had a wonderful visit in New York with my friend Norman Vincent Peale. He was eighty-two then.

---

* Helen Hayes, *Our Best Years* (Garden City, NY: Doubleday & Co., 1984), p. 138.

After we'd shared our faith and encouraged each other, we got down on our knees for a time of prayer. When we finished, I said, "That was great! Why don't we form a covenant to pray for each other every day wherever we are in the world?"

"Wonderful," Norman replied with gusto. "Let's make it for twenty years!"

"But Norman," I said, "you'll be a hundred and two years old then."

"That's right," he rejoined, "and I'll need your prayers then more than ever!"

Free of the past and filled with expectation for the future, Norman is a spontaneous person, open to live fully in the now.

Last summer I was with the Peales at the Tabernacle in Ocean City, New Jersey. I preached in the morning and Norman in the evening. After the evening service where Dr. Peale preached Christ with great power, I escorted his wife, Ruth, to a room while Norman greeted some of the thronging crowd that had come to hear him. When we were alone, she turned to me and said with radiant enthusiasm, "Lloyd, isn't he wonderful? Imagine, preaching the gospel like that at eighty-three!"

I agreed and thought to myself, "Now I know part of the secret of Norman's success: his trust in the Lord *and* Ruth's unbounding freedom to be an affirmer." Later, I thought about the people in my life who might need to know that I think they are wonderful. I made a list and the next day I phoned several and wrote others.

But how often we put off those spontaneous urgings. We stifle the childlike freedom in us and shrivel up inside and become unexpressive, dull people on the outside. The good news is that we don't have to stay that way.

The Desire for Life

Another important trait of children is that they feel free to express their desires. They are not self-sufficient, and they know it. It's only when we become adults that we hide our real needs and project an outer surface of adequacy.

I believe that one of the things Jesus appreciated about the boy in the crowd was that he really wanted to be with Him. The Master honors the honest expression of our needs. He longs for us to want His love, peace, and power because only then are we open to all He has in store for us.

How can we claim that? Christ's response to us is the same as it was to the disciples that day in Capernaum. "Unless you are converted and become as little children, you will by no means enter the kingdom of heaven." Kingdom life is the full, abundant life Jesus came to reveal and which He invites us to enjoy without reservation now and forever. The phrases "unless you are converted" and "become as little children" are two parts of this dynamic process. The first is done to and in us, and the second we do in response. Allow me to explain what I mean.

The word "converted" means to turn. In the verse we are considering, the Greek word is *straphēte,* the aorist passive subjective of *strephō,* meaning "to turn around."

Pardon me for bringing in a bit of Greek grammar. I think it will deepen our appreciation of this magnificent promise. The passive form of *strephō* can be translated literally as "to be turned around." A passive verb in Greek, as in English, indicates an action which is done to or for us. So the phrase "Unless you are converted" may imply that someone else does the converting or turning. Who does this for us? The Lord. He injects in us a dissatisfaction with life as we know it and then creates in us a desire for the quality of life He offers to us.

Conversion is a gift. It is a total redirection, a complete change of mind, a transformation of our personalities, and the reorientation of our wills. Conversion is a miracle of the Lord's grace. It begins with His choice of us. He singles us out to be the recipients of His love and forgiveness and then works through the circumstances of our lives to bring us to a realization that the life we are living is a grim substitute for the full-orbed joy He wants us to have. Graciously, He convicts us of the sin of our independence from Him and all we have done to cripple ourselves and hurt others.

A longing desire to know and love Him begins to grow in us as a direct result of His persistent movement in our minds. This brings us to repentance of our emptiness, our failure to live to the fullest, and our own inability to change ourselves. That's when we are given the magnificent endowment of faith to claim Christ's forgiveness through the atonement of the Cross and the power of His Resurrection as the assurance of His presence with us and of our participation in eternal life. Then, the same Lord who has brought us through the process of turning us around from self-centered ambition to complete trust in Him, actually comes to live in us as the new people He's enabled us to be. Dwelling within us He continues His transformation of making us like Himself!

The other day a man asked me when I was converted. My response was, "In May of 1949, repeatedly through the years, and most recently, yesterday." I went on to explain my initial turning to Christ as a college freshman, and my frequent need to turn anew whenever I have drifted from my love for, and obedience to, the Lord. In each of those times, He drew me back and created a fresh desire to live more fully in Him. Then I told the man about a relational problem I had faced the day before when a friend's attitudes brought me to the end of my patience. That had forced me to my knees and a deeper openness to what the Lord wanted me to be and do.

I'm not suggesting that conversion is something that is accomplished over a lifetime of effort in seeking to please the Lord. I believe that we should be able to identify the time when we were given the gift of faith to believe and the freedom to commit our lives to the Lord. Then the rest of life is a constant flow of renewal and growth.

That renewal and growth takes place as we consistently return to the childlike trust and spontaneity of this basic conversion. In this we have a choice. Jesus' phrase "become as little children" gives us the secret of living the adventure in Christ on a daily basis. The Greek word for "become" in this phrase is in the aorist but not the passive. Here it refers to a continuous, repetitive thing that we do, rather than something that's done to us. If we "keep on becoming" little children, then we realize in growing measure the growth in His greatness the Lord has prepared for us in the kingdom. Then the dynamic cycle is constantly repeated. And the gift of our initial conversion through the gift of childlike faith is renewed by a continuous series of conversions as we repeatedly choose to be childlike in our desire to be close to Christ.

A Scots pastor by the name of Ian Duncan never allows me to forget my need to keep alive the child in me as I grow in the Lord. We were fellow students at the University of Edinburgh years ago. When I'm in Scotland for my summer studies, I look him up and have a cup of tea with him. He's good for me.

Almost every year Ian asks, "Lloyd, are you movin' on with the Lord? That's the issue, isn't it? Are you more excited about the Lord and sharing His love than you were a year ago?"

My friend Ian believes that life in Christ should become more exciting year after year, and so do I. Each time he's asked, my grateful response has been an enthusiastic "Yes!"

Childlike Dependence

Often it's in the problems I face that I'm brought back to childlike dependence on the Lord and a desire to live spontaneously. And sometimes those problems threaten to make me take myself too seriously and not take the Lord's promises seriously enough. For a time, I try to work things out on my own strength. It never works. Then, when the tension becomes unbearable, the Lord turns my attention from the problem to Him and what He's done to help me in the past. My childlike trust is renewed, my basic conversion is rejuvenated and I feel fresh courage to go on. I'm free to live confidently again. As a result, a new childlike enthusiasm for the Lord, life, and people around me is released. The delight of life and the desire for more life is strong again. My will is strengthened. I find I have new will to turn to the Lord for His help.

When asked how she takes the immense problems of Calcutta, Mother Teresa responded, "I focus on the Lord and not the problems. Then I can deal with the problems holding the strong hand of Jesus."

Without a daily rebirth of the child and the continuous deepening of our conversion that provides, we'll all be "too soon old, too late free!"

10

WHEN
WE FEEL
MISUNDERSTOOD

WHEN POPE JOHN PAUL II visited New York, one of the rag sheets that masquerades as a newspaper ran the following headline: "The First Question the Pope Asked on Arriving in New York Was 'Are There Go-Go Girls in New York?'"

Behind that preposterous headline is a disturbing account which sharply focuses the problem of being misunderstood.

According to the story, the pope had been warned by his aides that newspaper reporters in New York might distort his words. That made him a bit wary in his first news conference after deplaning. The reporter representing this so-called newspaper asked the pope what he thought of the problem of "go-go" girls in New York. The pontiff hesitated and then asked, "Are there 'go-go' girls in New York?"

Most anyone in public life has experienced the pain and embarrassment of being misquoted. The mad scramble for the spectacular and for circulation often preys on careless or unscrupulous reporters whose concern is more for headlines than for truth. And while most of us may not be victimized by irresponsible media people searching for an attention-getting story that will sell, we frequently, in our personal relationships, confront a similar problem.

We all know the excruciating pain of being misunderstood and misrepresented. Often it's by people we love as well as by those we might consider less than friends. I think most of us try hard to say what we mean and mean what we say, but it is amazing sometimes what people hear. Communication has been defined as the "ground of meeting," but frequently in our conversations we miss, rather than meet.

How often we've heard it said or expressed it ourselves: "If I've told you once, I've told you a thousand times!" That's not only an exasperated complaint. It's a confession of our inability to really communicate effectively. Two things probably have contributed to this. First, we may not have expressed ourselves clearly, and, second, the listener may not have been listening. His or her attention may have been diverted by something else. But that doesn't let us off the hook. It's our responsibility to find ways of capturing people's attention and then, when we have it, to speak in ways that will be understood.

Most of us have a real problem with that. We are jolted when another person tells us what he or she thinks we've said, but has missed our meaning. How many times we've responded, "But that's not what I said!" And we are jolted even further when the other person responds, "I don't know what you meant to say, but that's what *I* heard!"

Then, at times the problem becomes all the more troublesome when a third person repeats back to us something we said to a mutual friend and then tells us that we were badly misunderstood. When this happens, we often blame others when the fault may be ours in not expressing ourselves clearly.

Some years ago, CBS executive Robert Tamplin invited me to a taping of "All in the Family" at the network studios here in Hollywood. In the particular episode being taped, Archie Bunker accused his wife Edith of not listening on his level. With his typical arrogance, Archie said, "The reason you don't understand me, Edith, is because I am talking in English and you are listening in dingbat!"

But whether we think we are communicating in English and people are listening in their own brand of "dingbat," communication is still one of our greatest problems.

Often, like Archie, we cover up our feelings of being misunderstood or unappreciated with so-called clever remarks that are really put-downs. A good example of this is in a reported conversation between Winston Churchill and Lady Astor at a dinner party. At one point Lady Astor said, "Winston, if you were my husband, I should flavor your coffee with poison." Quick as a flash Churchill responded, "Madam, if I were your husband, I should drink it!"

Then there was that massive put-down in the movie *Casablanca* when Peter Lorre said to Humphrey Bogart, "You despise me, don't you?" Bogart's memorable retort was, "Well, if I gave you any thought, I probably would."

But exchanges like that are not limited to historical figures or screen dialogue. They occur all too often in real life. Sometimes we say them and other times we are cut by them.

The other day in a restaurant I overheard a wife say to her husband, "We are passing each other like ships in the night. You say you understand what you think I'm saying, but what you are hearing is not what I'm saying!"

We've all felt like that and chances are we've all had some rendition of these words said to us. Our efforts to get through to people often are a combination of what we really want to say, what we actually say, what others hear, what they tell us they've heard, and our distressed reaction to what they didn't hear. And then we explode with, "You weren't listening to me!"

And so, we spend a lot of time trying to clean up misunderstandings and disappointments rooted in an inability to communicate, and in other people's perception of what we are trying to say. We find it difficult to express our true thoughts and deepest feelings in ways that will be heard and understood.

The problem of feeling misunderstood has profound implications not only for our daily conversations, but also for our efforts to share our faith. The chances are good that people will listen to our witness about what Christ means to us only if they have felt heard and understood, and if we have been effective in communicating affirmation and acceptance to them.

Facing the problem of misunderstandings is one thing; knowing what to do about it is something else. But eventually we have to come to the place where, instead of stewing over being misunderstood, we seek the Lord's help in becoming a person who communicates in the most effective way. After all, it is quite likely that we are misunderstood at times because we are not understandable!

A Promise for the Problem of Being Misunderstood

The Lord has made us an awesome promise for those times when we're misunderstood. It was first given to His followers as the assurance of His power when they would be put on trial because of their faith in Him. The promise is equally applicable for our conversations as it is for our ministry of communicating our faith. It is crucial for anyone who wants to talk in a way that will be understood.

After Jesus had explained that His followers would be brought before the synagogues, kings, and rulers for His sake, He made this promise, "But it will turn out for you as an occasion for testimony. Therefore settle it in your hearts not to meditate beforehand on what you will answer; for I will give you a mouth and wisdom which all your adversaries will not be able to contradict or resist" (Luke 21:13–15).

Most of us will not be "tried" for our faith, but we do face trying relationships. When misunderstandings occur we can claim that the Lord will use them for what He called

"an occasion for testimony." For us today, that means that
He will help us handle misunderstandings in a way that shows
others His grace at work in us. Because of His love for us,
we are freed from either self-pity or blaming others when misunderstandings occur. We can readily admit what we might
have done to cause a breakdown of communication and express
our desire to really listen to people. We don't always have
to be right or win every argument. Our openness and flexibility
will impress people and may give us an opportunity to share
our faith with them. Since feeling misunderstood is such a
distressing problem for most people, causing grief and unhappi-
ness, showing them Christ's method of dealing with conflict
will be a powerful witness.

Note the progression in the Lord's promise of how to do
that. We are told what not to do before we speak, what He
will give us while we are speaking, and what He will do to
help others understand what we say.

Freedom from Conning and Canning

First we are told not to meditate beforehand about what
we will say. That sounds like lack of preparation and clear
thinking about what we say in our conversations or sharing
of our faith. But look more closely at the Greek word Luke
uses for "meditate beforehand." It is *promeletaō*, "to con a
speech before it is given." To con means to study and investi-
gate. Did Jesus mean that we are not to prepare for what we
are going to say? Aren't we to do our homework in preparation
for our encounters with people?

Yes and no. Yes, we are to be prepared by His work in us
that shapes our character, personality, beliefs, and values. Yes,
we are to know who we are and where we are going because
of His liberating love and guidance within us. Yes, we are
to be honest and open with others about our convictions and
not equivocate.

But no, we are not to spend endless hours rehearsing what
we are going to say to a person. That kind of conning comes

off canned and superficial. It comes off as if we are more concerned about what we are going to say than the person to whom we are going to say it. Our agenda, not theirs, becomes uppermost in our minds.

Have you lain awake at night going over what you are going to say to a person the next day? Or have you ever sat scheming for hours how you would word what you were going to tell someone? Then, have you ever found that what you prepared didn't fit? Often we blurt out our carefully prepared statements with little sensitivity about how the person is feeling at that moment. It isn't a bit surprising that we are misunderstood so often.

The only way to avoid that is to trust Christ for the special kind of preparation He provides us for resolving misunderstandings. That preparation is happening all the time. Everything we go through prepares us for solving future problems. Daily prayer and Bible study condition our thinking and attitudes. Experience of the Lord's gracious patience with us makes us more sensitive to the needs in others. The Lord is constantly teaching us in the ups and downs of life. He knows the future and is getting us ready for what He knows is ahead of us.

When a misunderstanding disturbs us we can spread it out before the Lord. He will direct our thinking to passages of Scripture which reveal His truth. He will remind us of what we've learned from Him in similar conflicts. And He will give us profound, forgiving love for the people who are troubling us. We will be given a new empathy to sense what may be causing the people involved in the misunderstanding to talk and act in ways which have hurt us. It's then that we can commit the outcome to the Lord, trusting Him completely.

The result of this preparation is that we are set free of the need to justify ourselves with defensive statements. We can enter into conversation with people who have hurt us, be prepared to listen attentively, and when the timing is right, respond spontaneously, drawing on all the Lord has done to prepare our thinking and attitudes.

What Father John Powell prays before giving a talk could

well be our preparation for attempts to straighten out misunderstandings. "May what I say be less of a presentation and more of an act of love."

Often, when my wife, Mary Jane, knows that I have a misunderstanding to work out on a particular day, before I leave home in the morning she asks, "Lloyd, are you prepared?" I know she is not referring to the preparation of a canned monologue or well-rehearsed phrases, but the preparation of quiet with the Lord. Years of working with people have taught both of us that we can't make it without that!

The same is true for opportunities to share our faith. The Lord prepares us for what He has prepared. The way He helps us in our troubles prepares us for the troubled people we meet who desperately need His love and power. Here again canned speeches miss the mark. People are put off when we shift into the honed phrases of overused jargon. But when we really listen intently to people's problems we will discover we've been through the same or similar difficulties. Then we can draw from our own real life experiences of how the Lord stepped in to help us. That usually gives us an opportunity to help people to commit not only their specific problem, but their whole lives, to the Lord.

After a time like that we look back and realize we could not have been effective communicators without the training in living the Lord had allowed in our lives.

And we are aware of something else. We were not alone. The Lord was there with us guiding exactly what we were to say. That's the confidence of the second part of the promise we are considering.

A Mouth and Wisdom

When we attempt to share our faith or heal misunderstandings the Lord promises that He will give us "a mouth and wisdom." The word mouth, *stoma* in Greek, is used figuratively for speech. Wisdom, *sophia*, refers to the mind of the

Lord that is given to us for particular people and circumstances. That's a great two-part offer for our efforts to be effective communicators. The Lord will guide our thoughts for what needs to be said and He will give us the most effective way of saying it. When we pray constantly during an exchange with a person, the Lord will actually speak through us. Mark's rendering of Jesus' promise is ". . . do not worry beforehand, or premeditate what you will speak. But whatever is given you in that hour, speak that; for it is not you who speak, but the Holy Spirit" (Mark 13:11).

I know firsthand how the Lord keeps that promise—both to enable truly effective conversation and to help people with their problems. So often the Lord gives me on-the-spot insight and discernment to express something I knew He was guiding me to say. An insight, a verse of Scripture, an experience, or a carefully timed challenge was exactly what a person needed at that moment. What a joy it is to learn, sometimes long afterward, that what I felt led to say was liberating to a person.

I wish I could say that is always the case. But sometimes, like all of us, I get in the way and say things I wish later I could retract. But the Lord is ready to help me even then. This happened to me not long ago when I became upset by something Al, one of the elders in my church, said in a meeting. His words sounded like an attack on my judgment. And without thinking or praying I responded sharply and defensively. Fortunately, we both had the good sense to let the matter drop and not ruin the whole meeting. Unfortunately, however, we were not able to talk after the meeting and both of us went home brooding over the misunderstanding.

The next morning, when I awoke, Al was on my mind. The Lord clearly gave me orders to call my friend before that day ended. I resisted the temptation to plan what I would say. All I was to do was call, reaffirm our friendship in Christ, apologize for being so defensive, ask Al to tell me what he was trying to say, and then keep my mouth shut and listen.

When I called Al in the afternoon, he said, "I'm so glad you called. I had a restless night and you've been on my mind all day." He had reflected on the confrontive way he had expressed himself and was sorry for the tension it had caused. Then he went on to explain what was really behind his comments. It was not meant to be an attack on my judgment at all. In fact, when he clarified what he really meant, it was an insight I needed to hear. I thanked him, and we ended the conversation deeper friends than before.

Think of what might have happened without that Spirit-guided conversation. I could easily have labeled Al as an obstructionist or a negative critic and imprisoned him with that judgment for months, even years. And of course, our friendship would have become strained and our leadership in the church rendered far less effective. Instead, the Lord intervened to give both of us a "mouth and wisdom" to speak and hear truth from each other.

Sometimes the word the Lord gives us to communicate is a genuine apology. Recently, Sam, a fellow pastor who is a prayer partner, wrote me about a very crucial project for which he wanted my public support. His letter and proposal arrived the day after I had left for two weeks' vacation Upon my return, I found the material and notes of his repeated calls, but a demanding crisis occupied my attention for another week. I should have called him immediately, regardless of other pressures. What I had failed to grasp was that the request had been waiting two weeks before I even saw it. Finally I dropped everything and placed a call to Sam.

With legitimate coolness, he said, "Lloyd, it's been three weeks! I've put hundreds of hours into this project, and you of all people, a close friend and prayer partner have taken all this time to respond!"

As my friend poured out his disappointment and hurt, I asked the Lord to give me a "mouth and wisdom." I had failed my friend and had to admit it. The best thing I could do now was listen.

It was well into the conversation when my friend said, "This is so unlike you. There must be some explanation. Are you all right?" Only then did the Lord release me to offer an explanation. Aching inside, I told Sam I understood what he was feeling and that he was more than justified. All I could do was ask for forgiveness, rather than keep harping on the combination of circumstances that had caused my seeming neglect and insensitivity. The conversation ended with Sam's assuring words, "Lloyd, I forgive you and want to put this behind me completely so we can press on." When I hung up the phone, I thanked the Lord for guiding me and my friend through the troubled waters of misunderstanding.

Things like that happen to all of us. We do things wittingly and unwittingly which contradict our best intentions and the expectations we have for ourselves and others have for us. This sort of thing happens in our marriages, among our friends, and in the fellowship of the church. The problem is not just in the turbulence of misunderstanding, but so often in not allowing the Lord to guide us in seeking for, or being open to give forgiveness and experience reconciliation.

Abraham Lincoln was told that Secretary Stanton had called him a fool. Lincoln responded with grace, "I want to have a talk with him because he's usually right." There's an excellent model for us when we feel misunderstood.

Anointed Listeners

I believe we are not only to pray for guidance for what we do or do not say, but for the listening capacity of those with whom we're trying to communicate. The third part of Jesus' promise in Luke 21:13–15 is that He will overcome the "contradictions and resistance" of those to whom we speak. That's particularly encouraging for the times when we are under fire for what we believe. But it is also a comforting assurance in resolving conflicts. It is our challenge to be as straightforward as possible and depend on the Lord to enable people both to hear what we say and what we really mean.

Getting through to other people, with all that's going on in their minds, is little short of a miracle. Hearing is an amazing process. The sounds of our words must be registered on the eardrum and passed through the auditory nerves through to the brain. But how these sounds are registered depends on what is going on in people's thinking. What they hear is dramatically affected by their preconceptions and prejudices.

That's why it is important to pray during our efforts to resolve misunderstandings. A prayerful attitude opens people up to what we are trying to communicate. It also keeps us from coming across as if everything we say is a direct word from the Lord. Few things jam the communication lines more than saying, "I've talked to the Lord about you and this is what He told me to tell you that you ought to do!" Instead, we are to share truth as it has become real to us in our own experience—with love.

But what about those people who hear clearly and still choose to misunderstand us?

Understanding Doesn't Always Lead to Understanding

Eventually we have to grapple with the fact that not all misunderstandings are a lack of understanding. Most of the time we use the understanding for both comprehension and acceptance. But, let's face it, there are times when people hear what we are saying, understand it perfectly, and still do not accept it.

Jesus follows up His promise for effective communication with a note of reality. In Luke 21:15–19 He clearly states that His followers will experience misunderstanding from their families, relatives, and friends because of their commitment to Him. This adds a note of honest realism about our efforts to communicate. We're not going to get everyone to agree with us. In fact, we will face irreconcilable differences with some people because they have heard what we have said and simply disagree or forcefully oppose what they hear.

Not Simplistic

The fact that sometimes people do not agree with our views is not a contradiction of Jesus' bold promise about effective communication, but a liberating assurance, for we are set free from the simplistic idea that all our efforts to heal misunderstandings will be successful. Our purpose is to be faithful to the Lord, be as clear about our convictions as we can be with His help, and be persistent at efforts for resolving misunderstandings. But if we fail to achieve understanding we must not condemn ourselves. There are too many people ready to hear and really understand for us to spend our creative energies in remorse over those who refuse. And don't forget—the Lord is amazingly resourceful—He will find someone else to get through to those with whom we have been unable to communicate. Our challenge is to be faithful, not always successful by our standards.

When we are faithful we often discover that what seems to be a rejection is really an honest disagreement. That may be only a stage of serious consideration of what we are trying to communicate.

Sincere Disagreements

Recently I had to relearn the truth that sincere disagreements are part of life. A certain woman in our church didn't like it because I gave an invitation for people to come forward for prayer with the elders at the end of our Sunday morning services. Olivia just wasn't impressed by either the dedication of the elders who met with people to pray or the results that occurred in the lives of people. It just was not "Presbyterian," she insisted. "We don't need that kind of emotional response on Sunday morning."

Olivia made her objection clearly known around the congregation. She got my attention. I asked to see her and opened the conversation by saying, "We have a misunderstanding and I'd like to talk about it." She responded by saying flatly, "There's no misunderstanding. I understand exactly what you are doing and the reasons you've explained repeatedly, and I'm in complete disagreement and opposition! It's just not Presbyterian!" I then asked her to explain what she meant by Presbyterian. She replied by talking about the customs and traditions to which she had become accustomed as a member of several other Presbyterian churches in various cities where she and her family had lived.

After Olivia had talked at length, I tried to explain the prayerful thinking that went into the process of the elders praying with and for people. The decision had been made "decently and in order" to use an old Presbyterian phrase. But nothing I said convinced Olivia, and we agreed to disagree.

Paul, an elder who was a close friend of Olivia and her husband, picked up where I left off. He listened as a friend to her objections, but also stood firm in his belief that what we were doing was biblical and guided by the Lord.

Sometime later, Olivia's younger brother became seriously ill, and she was deeply distressed. One evening after dinner together with Olivia and her husband, Paul and his wife heard about the brother's illness and Olivia's concern. This was the first time Olivia had expressed any kind of personal need to her friends. And in response, Paul asked if he and his wife could pray for the brother. They did, and Olivia was greatly blessed as she felt the caring concern of loving friends.

At the end of the evening together, Paul tenderly said to Olivia, "Dear friend, the kind of prayer we've had tonight for your brother is no different from what we offer at the end of services on Sunday morning." Now Olivia was more ready to understand, but Paul was wise enough not to press the matter. He knew that the door to Olivia's heart had been opened just a bit.

Over the next months, Olivia observed more closely those who came forward for prayer at the end of our services. She felt a growing compassion for them because of her own need. And then one morning I was the most surprised and delighted person in the sanctuary when she came forward for prayer for her brother. I'm happy to say that the Lord answered those prayers by healing both the brother and Olivia's rigid resistance to the elders' efforts to make our congregation a truly caring, praying church.

I've told Olivia's story because it reveals how the Lord works through circumstances and other people even after we think we have failed in a misunderstanding. The Lord is showing me that the battle for truth is His battle. And He is very original in the ways He can get His work done through others when I think I've failed in getting agreement with complete understanding.

Eight Keys of Communication

I want to close this part of our discussion by sharing with you eight discoveries about relationships and communication with others that have helped me.

1. People do not care about how much we know until they know how much we care. Deep communication is possible only as we help people to know and feel our affirmation and concern for them. It is what *we are* and what *we do* to express love that creates a climate for openness for what we say.

2. People will understand what we say only after they know we understand them. That means taking them seriously in the expression of their ideas, values, hopes, and dreams, as well as their needs, problems, and distresses. Other people will accept what we say only as they feel accepted. Our tendency is not to see things as they are, but as *we* are. Walter Lippmann said, "We all are captives of the pictures in our heads—our belief that the world we have experienced is the world that really exists." And we've got to get into that world!

3. People will listen only when we've taken time to listen to them. Active listening requires discipline. Usually we are thinking so much about what we are going to say when it's our turn to speak that we don't really hear what the other person has said. Listening demands attention, the focus of all our faculties, plus our body language and eye contact, so that people know we have really zeroed in on them completely.

4. People are like harbors and each is his or her own harbor-master. They must provide us with the charts to know how to find the channel and come into port and dock on the landing of their interests and needs. Most people are concerned about themselves and what they are experiencing. But when they feel we care about them, they will open up. That earns us the right to be heard when we speak.

5. People can hear six times faster than we can talk. So when it's our turn in a conversation, get to the point! The average speaker can say about 125 words a minute and the average listener can process over 600 words a minute. It's what happens in the intervals while we drone on that usually loses our listener.

6. People will misunderstand. Three elements are involved in every conversation: the one who speaks, what is said, and the person who listens. We can depend on Christ to help us with all three. When misunderstandings do occur, pray before and during attempts to straighten things out.

7. People are slow to admit they were wrong or precipitous in their judgments. For this reason, the ball is always in our court as a part of our ministry of reconciliation. It's a misnomer to say, "Time will heal this misunderstanding." Sometimes a lapse of time only solidifies people's opinions and feelings of hurt. When we ask the Lord for help, He will guide our timing. He's usually ready long before we are. When He gives the signal, our task is to go to the person with an open, receptive attitude, listen to his or her feelings and complaints, and then lovingly communicate that more than being right we desire reconciliation.

8. People will not always respond to our best efforts. Honor their right to continue to misunderstand you. When your convictions and integrity are involved, don't change who you are just to please. Release the person from having to agree with you. The last chapter of his or her life and of your relationship has not been written. Surrender the unresolved misunderstanding to the Lord and leave it with Him.

These eight reminders have become a part of a covenant between the Lord and me for more effective communication. I typed them out when I had one of those days in which I had to deal with several misunderstandings. I keep them in my Bible for a daily reminder.

One of the most astounding ambiguities of our human nature is that, knowing how much it hurts when we are misunderstood, we willfully contribute to misunderstandings in our relationships with others. I have decided to do all I can, whenever I can, with whomever I can, to overcome the misunderstandings of life. I invite you to join me in that difficult, often thankless, but ultimately rewarding adventure.

11

THE
PROBLEM OF
ANSWERED PRAYER

WE HEAR A LOT ABOUT what seems to be unanswered prayer. Hardly a day goes by that someone doesn't share with me the frustration that either God has not heard or hasn't responded to his or her prayers. We all want guidance, wisdom, and power from God. We want to know that He hears and cares and answers our petitions. So we cry out, "Lord, grant me the desires of my heart, show me what You want me to do, bless me and my loved ones, but please Lord, don't be silent!" Who hasn't had the experience of what appears to be unanswered prayer?

But one day while reading the responses to the questionnaire I had sent out asking people to send me a list of their biggest problems, I was startled by one person's response card. Printed out on the card were five words in bold letters. They were underlined with urgency and had an exclamation point at the end for emphasis: *The problem of answered prayer!*

I sat back in my chair and spent a long time thinking about this unusual expression of need. Not unanswered prayer but answered prayer! How could receiving an answer to our prayers be a problem?

The more I thought about this, the more I realized that frequently answers to prayer are more challenging than coping with what we consider unanswered prayer. In fact, many times what we call unanswered prayer is really the problem of answered prayer. There are times, I'm sure, that we concentrate so hard on asking for something that we are insensitive to the answer when it comes. And often answers to prayer are more than we bargained for. Or it comes in a different way than we expected. Then, there are times when the answer presents us with a challenge to become part of the answer.

Elizabeth Barrett Browning was on target with her arrow of truth about the problem of answered prayer.

> God answers sharp and sudden on some prayers,
> And thrusts the thing we've prayed for in our face,
> A gauntlet with a gift in it.*

It's recognizing and accepting the gauntlet and opening it to discover the gift that is the problem of answered prayer. Let's talk about that. I think we'll find that solving the problem of answered prayer will help us overcome what we may have mistakenly called unanswered prayer.

A Promise for the Problem of Answered Prayer

When we pray in Jesus' name, we can have the liberating assurance that all of our prayers will be answered. That's the essence of the promise Jesus gave His disciples when they were together in the upper room on the night before the crucifixion. The promise is nestled in among some very crucial teachings. He had told them He would soon be leaving them. But He was coming back. He would manifest Himself to them.

---

* From *Aurora Leigh*, Elizabeth Barrett Browning, Second Book, line 952.

Jesus also made it clear that night that prayer would be the vital, enabling link between Him and them. And most important of all, He would be the instigator of their desire to pray; the interpreter of the best way for those prayers to be answered for the ultimate good of all concerned; and the implementer of that answer in their lives. All of these dynamic elements are contained in Christ's awesome promise, "And whatever you ask in My name, that I will do, that the Father may be glorified in the Son. If you ask anything in My name, I will do it" (John 14:13–14).

Now, Jesus didn't say, "If you ask for whatever you want, it will be done for you." But He did promise that He would answer all prayers prayed in His name.

To pray in Jesus' name is to pray for what is in keeping with His plan, purpose, and power. That is both comforting and challenging. When we pray in His name, we have the promise that all our prayers are heard and reviewed by His sovereign authority. Only what will accomplish His plan for us is granted. He is our compassionate, but all-knowing and all-loving prayer censor. As such, He answers our prayers with His all-wise yes, no, or later. Some prayers are answered with the blessing and guidance we've asked for. Others, which would not be best for us are refused. And other answers are delayed because the timing is not right or we are not ready.

Does that give you a tremendous sense of relief? It does me! We can pray with freedom and joy knowing that the Master Strategist is sorting out our prayers and managing His answers for our growth and His glory in our lives. His granting what we seek, His denials, or His delays are all answers to our prayers. But from our point of view, accepting what He knows is best isn't always easy for us. That's the problem of answered prayer.

There are three kinds of answers to prayer which cause us difficulty: those we are reluctant to acknowledge, those we resist, and those we are tempted to refuse. Let's consider these in the light of Jesus' promise in John 14:13–14.

Unacknowledged Answers to Prayer

We begin a day asking for the Lord's blessing. He answers by providing us with strength, guidance, and care. And yet, we fail so often to praise Him for His presence with us. We get caught up in the pressures of the day and forget that each breath we breathe, each beat of our pulse, every thought we think is an answer to our prayer at the beginning of the day. And we seem to forget that the Lord is constantly at work giving us exactly what we need.

We pray the Lord's Prayer with unthinking regularity. In the marvelous and inclusive prayer we ask for God's will to be done, for the provision of daily bread, for protection against evil and temptation. A thousand times every day our petitions are answered, but we are seldom as persistent in thanking the Lord as we have been in making our petitions.

Then at night we pray before going to sleep and ask the Lord to forgive the mistakes of the past day. We ask Him to pour out His blessings in the day ahead. Then all through the night He cares for us, healing the fatigue of our bodies, relieving our minds of tension, and refreshing us for the coming day. And yet, so often we awake in the morning and forget to praise the Lord for the answers to our prayers.

Most of our days begin without our giving any thought to the miracle of being alive. Instead of saying, "Good morning Lord, thanks for the day!" we often say, "Good lord, it's morning; another day!" Then as we move through the day, problems cloud our minds with dread. And we fret about them instead of expressing delight that the Lord will be in us to give us insight and wisdom to solve them.

In the hotel where I stay in Edinburgh, Scotland, during my summer study times, there's a cheery Scots woman by the name of Kathy. She's almost as wide as she is tall. Her hair is dyed carrot red. Even though she is in her late sixties, Kathy is a bundle of energy which she happily invests in her task of cleaning the guests' rooms and preparing their breakfasts.

One night I worked around the clock trying to finish my work before returning home. At five in the morning Kathy saw the light from my study lamp spilling into the corridor from the transom above the door to my room. Concerned, she rapped gently. When I opened the door she said, "Oh, Doctor, all this work is going to be the death o' ye. Have ye been up all night? Would ye like to have some breakfast to cheer ye on?" I agreed that breakfast would be very nice, suddenly realizing how hungry I was. Then, just before turning to go, Kathy smiled winsomely and asked, "Have ye heard God singin' this mornin'?"

I had to admit that I'd been too busy working for the Lord all night to hear Him singing. To that she replied, "It's in the Good Book, ye know. You're supposed to be a scholar. Know where it is? Look it up while I fix yer breakfast!" She turned and scurried off, humming joyously to herself.

I went back to my desk and quickly followed instructions. A verse memorized years before came to mind. I opened my Bible to Zephaniah 3:17: "The Lord your God in your midst, the Mighty One, will save; He will rejoice over you with gladness. He will quiet you in His love, He will rejoice over you with singing."

And there in the gray light of a new day I heard God singing. It was a song He placed in my heart. A song of rejoicing over His gracious presence and power, a song of gratitude that He'd helped me through the night. With that song of gladness ringing in me throughout the rest of the morning I finished my work with praise. Then the words of another favorite verse came to my mind: ". . . Because His compassions fail not. They are new every morning; great is Your faithfulness. 'The Lord is my portion,' says my soul, 'Therefore I hope in Him!'" (Lam. 3:22–24).

My day was completely changed because a Spirit-filled Scottish cook had reminded me that the Lord was singing over me! Amazing, isn't it? I had worked all night doing God's work without His joy. But when I paused with gratitude to acknowledge the answers to prayer I had already received, I was able to tackle some problems for which I thought I had had no answers. The answers had been there all along.

So, the first step in dealing with the problem of answered prayer is to begin thanking the Lord for all the blessings we receive every day but seldom acknowledge. Being thankful produces a tremendous change in us which frees us to confront the second part of our problem with answered prayer.

When the Answers Are Different Than We Expect

When a problem comes and we are worried about the outcome, our first desire is to tell the Lord what we think He should do. Even when we pray, "Your will be done, Lord; I will accept whatever is best for me," we have clear preconceptions about what that "best" ought to be. There are times, too, when we arrogantly tell the Lord what we want and when we want it! Now, added to whatever problem brought us to prayer is the bigger problem of trying to run our own lives. As a result, we are very resistant to answers which do not meet our specifications. Sometimes it takes us days, months, even years, to recognize the answer the Lord gives.

Ben, a friend of mine, was very emphatic when he said, "I've decided to stop praying! I've prayed and prayed about this problem and either God isn't listening or He's decided not to care about my needs."

"How would you know if He did answer you?" I asked.

"Well," Ben responded, "the problem would be solved!"

"What if the answer is different from what you expected? Would that still be an answer?"

After a long pause, Ben said, "I see what you mean. I guess I've been so settled on one thing as the answer that I really have not been open to anything else. Are you suggesting that the way this thing has worked out may be the answer and I've refused to accept it?"

"Exactly!" I said. "You may be resisting the answer not only because it's not what you wanted, but because you still want to run your own life. Can you dare to believe that God knows what He's doing and that what He grants or withholds is according to a wise plan for your life?"

That led to a thoughtful conversation. At the end of our visit, Ben decided that he needed a much deeper relationship with the Lord. What he had missed were prolonged times in prayer in which he attempted to discover what to pray for. Ben had been so busy giving orders to the Lord that he had not allowed the Lord to help him formulate his prayers according to God's will.

Pann Baltz's story provides a vivid contrast to Ben's problem with answered prayer. The Lord answered Pann's prayers for healing differently than she had hoped—at first.

Pann is a young mother who has struggled with the problem of answered prayer and has won. Some time ago, I asked her to share her witness with our congregation. It was the day before her birthday. Here is what she said with radiance and amazing joy.

"Tomorrow is my birthday and there are many reasons why I'll be celebrating this birthday with particular joy. Last year I spent my birthday in the intensive care unit, and I didn't think I ever wanted to have a birthday again.

"Life just seemed too difficult. In the last two-and-a-half years I have had nine strokes and I've spent sixteen months in the hospital. I've had numerous surgeries, been on a respirator many times, and had two cardiac arrests. With each stroke I've been paralyzed on the right side and at times I've lost my ability to speak, to read, or to see well.

"They tell me that medically I should be dead. But for God's reasons I am alive and today I am praising Him for what I call His walking, talking, reading, and writing miracles of life in me.

"Emotionally, I'll be celebrating because now I want to live. Many times during my illnesses I really wanted to die.

Negative feelings of anger, fear, disappointment, and depression overwhelmed me. But God's been teaching me—through a study of David's feelings in the Psalms and through the wise counsel of Christian friends—to give these feelings to Him. And I have discovered that when I give all my feelings, both positive and negative, to the Lord, He not only listens and understands, but He heals the hurting feelings as well.

"Spiritually I'll be celebrating because now there is a peace within me. When I first became ill, I had a close relationship with the Lord. But as the illness dragged on for months and years it became hard for me to believe that God was working in my life. Although there were armies of people praying for me, I was still sick.

"Then in January of this year I had a real inner healing from the Lord. I felt at that time He assured me it was His will for me to be a completely whole person. I don't know if that means I will have a complete physical recovery from all my illness and the paralysis that still affects me, but I do know that my body is no mystery to the Lord and He is working within me.

"And the Lord also gave me a promise from Isaiah, 'Cease to dwell on days gone by, and to brood over past history. Here and now I will do a new thing. This moment it will break from the bud. Can you not perceive it? I will make a way even in the wilderness' (Isa. 43:18–19).

"God has been true to that promise. He's been with me in my wilderness, and I know He'll be with me in any wilderness that faces me in the future. And I've been healed within, which is the most important healing of all.

"Today my prayer of praise to the Lord is found in the words of the Psalmist, 'Lord, be thou my helper. Thou hast turned my laments into dancing, Thou has stripped off my sackcloth and clothed me with joy, that my spirit may sing psalms to Thee, and never cease. I will confess Thee forever, O Lord my God' " (Psalms 30:10–12).

This courageous woman has been given the gift of being

able to trust the Lord with her life, even though His answer
came differently than she expected. But wrapped up in the
answer were blessings she probably would never have known
without complete trust and unreserved surrender.

In praying for physical problems in myself and others, I've
had to learn that the Lord works out His plan and purpose
in many different ways. Sometimes, I am amazed at how
quickly the Lord gives physical healing. Our temptation is
to expect that the Lord will deal with everyone as He has
with some. Not so. With tender compassion and sublime wisdom, He cares for each one personally, producing first an inner,
spiritual healing. And whether or not we are healed physically,
the Lord wants us to receive the gift of deeper faith and re-
silient courage and freedom to praise Him for His strength.

We experience some of these same results when we pray
for problems in our relationships. We pray for people and
often the outcome is very different than what we anticipated.
A Lutheran pastor friend named Lee is a good example of
this.

I first met Lee at a conference at Stanford University. He
was very discouraged about his church. Many of the church's
two hundred members were very resistant to renewal and Lee's
efforts to lead them into being a dynamic congregation. As
we talked, I became very impressed with Lee and the Christ-
like style of his leadership. At the conclusion of the visit, I
felt prompted to say a rather daring thing, "Lee, I really affirm
what you're attempting to do. I know you're being held back
by obstructionists. Why don't you begin praying, 'Lord, revive
them or remove them!' "

Lee went back to his church committed to continue preaching Christ and giving courageous leadership in the development of a New Testament quality church. His daily prayer
about those who were barricading his ministry was that the
Lord would either change them or that they would change
churches. He fully expected that the Lord would change the
people and their attitudes.

Guess what? In that next year one hundred of the two hundred members left the church. This wasn't at all what Lee had anticipated. But the Lord knew what He was doing. He pruned out the dead wood. The obstructionists drifted to other more traditional, less challenging congregations. Then with a hundred deeply committed, willing, and ready members, the Lord began to rebuild. And the results far exceeded Lee's expectations.

Recently I saw Lee and he told me that now, a few years after praying that daring "revive them or remove them" prayer, his congregation numbers over two thousand!

I'm sure that during these black days when certain people were leaving and his congregation was cut in half that Lee agonized over the seeming loss. It would have been so easy for him to become defensive, self-critical, or question what the Lord was doing. But what might have seemed to be the end of a very promising ministry was really just the beginning. And Lee had to live with raw trust through the process.

When We Are Called to Be Part of the Answer

Now we come to the third aspect of the problem of answered prayer: How do we respond when the Lord involves us in the answer? It is one thing to turn a problem over to the Lord; it is quite something else when He conscripts us to be His partner in the solution.

Betty discovered that being a part of the solution was her problem with answered prayer. For years she prayed for her husband, Jim, to become a Christian. But as the years of praying dragged by, she developed a kind of false security expressed in a feeling of spiritual superiority. She rather enjoyed being the one who knew God and guided the spiritual development of their four children. At the same time, though, she continued praying that Jim would become a Christian.

When Betty's prayers were answered, she was not as pleased as she thought she would be. Jim made a profound

commitment to Christ, joined the church, and wanted to
share the adventure of his new faith with Betty. Now she
was faced with giving up her lever of superiority. For a time
she struggled to accept the answer to her prayers. Finally she
told the Lord about that struggle and asked for His help.

Again the Lord answered with more than she expected. But
this time she was ready. When her husband suggested daily
prayer together she responded with joy. Next, they joined a
couple's prayer and study group. Then they accepted a responsibility to be team-teachers of a church school class. And recently, they began to tithe. Day by day they are enjoying
greater love in their marriage than ever before. They are on
the move spiritually in a new partnership with each other
and the Lord.

Another way in which we are confronted with the problem
of answered prayer is when we pray for a person who distresses
us. In praying, we ask the Lord to change the person, but
often He involves us in the process.

One of the severe problems the early Christian church faced
was a person—Saul of Tarsus. He was a militant persecutor
of the Christians. Undoubtedly they prayed for the Lord's
intervention. Perhaps some of them even prayed for Saul. But
we wonder how many of them expected the Lord's answer
to their prayers. He moved in a dramatic way in Saul's conversion. But He involved one of the leaders among the Damascus
Christians in the process.

The Lord could have completed the conversion of Saul when
He appeared to the vigilant Pharisee on the road to Damascus.
Instead, He chose to act in a way that would both transform
Saul and release the church from its fear of him.

Luke tells us in Acts that Saul was blinded as a result of
his initial encounter with the Lord. Not being able to see,
Saul was led by his soldiers to a house in Damascus on the
street called Straight. There, alone in his darkness, Saul was
left to contemplate what had happened to him. Could it be
that the same Christ whom he persecuted by purging the

church was no dead Galilean, but was the risen, living Lord?

When the Lord knew that Saul was ready, He appeared to Saul again. This time to tell him that a Christian, Ananias, would come, lay his hands on him, and his blindness would be healed. Ananias? He had probably been on the top of Saul's hit list for Damascus.

We can only imagine the panic Ananias expressed when the Lord also appeared to him and told him to go to Saul of Tarsus and lay hands on him and confirm his conversion. "Saul of Tarsus, Lord? He's the one who is on his way to destroy the church! How could you want me to extend love and blessing to our archenemy?" Ananias was face to face with a problem of answered prayer.

The conversation between the Lord and Ananias must have taken longer than the brief synopsis Luke records in Acts 9:10–16. What we do know is that Ananias obeyed and went to Saul. His opening words communicate the love the Lord had given him to replace his fear, anger, and panic. "Brother Saul," Ananias said with compassion and reconciling grace.

The Lord honored that costly obedience and with the laying on of Ananias's hands He confirmed Saul's calling, healed him, and filled him with His Spirit.

As a further act of healing, Ananias introduced Saul to the very church in Damascus he had come to stamp out. Think of what it must have meant for the Christians to break bread and drink from a common cup in Communion with Saul who a few days before had been a feared enemy. In startling ways the Lord involved the early Christians in the answer to their prayers for deliverance from Saul's persecution. In Acts 9:31 we read of His full answer to that prayer after Saul's conversion. "Then the churches throughout all Judea, Galilee, and Samaria had peace. . . ."

This truth causes us to stop and think about people in our lives who are our enemies or who cause us difficulty. It is possible that praying for these people may bring us a greater challenge than we want. The Lord may be calling us to express love and forgiveness to those very people. The cost of answered prayer will be our obedience!

The same thing is true for our concern over social problems in the cities in which we live. We pray for the hungry, for those living in poverty, for the disadvantaged, or for social conditions which need to be changed. But a part of the Lord's answer may be to involve us in giving our money and time to be His agents of social change in the very problems about which we have prayed.

This is happening to people in our church. As a result of concern for the problems in Hollywood and the greater Los Angeles community, many of them have become prayer warriors for the Lord's victory over the forces of social evil. But those prayers have often been answered by a call to obedience to become actively involved in the solution He guides. The Lord's challenge to Israel during the exile in Jeremiah chapter twenty-nine has come alive with twentieth-century implications.

We have heard the Lord's call to become faithful servants to really care about our city. "Seek the welfare of the city where I have sent you . . . and pray to the Lord on its behalf, for in its welfare you will find your welfare" (Jer. 29:7, RSV).

When we accept that call we can realize the Lord's promise, "For I know the plans I have for you, says the Lord, plans for welfare and not for evil, to give you a future and a hope" (Jer. 29:11, RSV).

We are encouraged by the Lord's assurance that He will direct our activity as we seek to be part of His answer. And we are given confidence when we claim the further promise, "Then you will call upon me and come and pray to me, and I will hear you. You will seek me and find me; when you seek me with all your heart" (Jer. 29:12, RSV).

These dynamic assurances have given many of our members the courage to step out with boldness in their servant ministry. Thousands of volunteer hours are invested each year in being part of the Lord's answers to our prayers for community problems. I have come to believe that a growing, on-the-move Christian must have some specific ministry to bring Christ's love and renewal to our neighborhoods and cities. Our awareness of a need is the first part of the answer to prayer. When we are willing to be part of the Lord's solution, we are given the wisdom and strength to tackle what otherwise would seem to be impossible. That willingness is the secret of spiritual power—Christ's power in answer to our prayers.

Beyond Bartering for Blessing

When we finally believe that all prayers are answered, though sometimes differently than we expected and often involving us in the answer, we are freed from using prayer as a time of bartering for blessings. Or to put it more bluntly, we are freed from using prayer to send blackmail offers to the Lord. Whenever we promise the Lord that we will do, or stop doing something, if He will bless us with what we ask, we have lowered prayer to a bargaining session.

Often I hear people say that they will give up some habit or act differently in their relationships if the Lord will only hear and answer their prayers. This is a subtle kind of works-oriented self-justification. We make the Lord into a projected parent who will give us what we want if we behave. Or we relate to Him like a banker to whom we promise we will be more responsible in our financial affairs if he will make us the loan we want. And at best, we treat Him like a friend who always wants something from us in return for a favor.

The Lord of answered prayer is so much more than these. He wants to liberate us from this tendency to anthropopathy—projecting on Him the reactions of our humanness and expecting Him to react as we would.

If, as we pray, we are convicted about something we've done or are doing that makes us uncomfortable in the Lord's presence, that also may be part of answered prayer. Acting on that guidance will make us more receptive to the answers

He has waiting for us. But promising to change in order to get Him to act is evidence that we have not accepted His unconditional love and His unqualified desire to answer our prayers and involve us in accomplishing the answers.

Finally, the greatest answer to prayer is the Lord Himself. His will for us is an intimate relationship of profound trust. He has a plan for our lives that He longs to unfold for us. Consistent times in prayer enable us to know Him and what He wants us to do. But when we complain of unanswered prayer, we are really confessing that we haven't truly prayed. For when we want Him more than the answers we demand, we'll have the ultimate answer from which all lesser answers flow.

So, the so-called problem of answered prayer is not really a problem after all. Remember our definition of the word problem as something that stands in our way of making progress. An answer to prayer, though it is challenging and demanding, is given to open the way, not block it. Even when the answer is a closed door, we can know the Lord has another door open, waiting. And when we must wait for direction to that door, we know that the Lord's timing is perfect.

12

WHEN LIFE KICKS THE JOY OUT OF YOU

THERE'S A GLUM PROPRIETOR of a book and stationery store near the University of Edinburgh, Scotland. As I've visited the store over the years, I've noticed that the man's habitual response to his customers' question "How are you?" is always the same: "About as good as can be expected under the circumstances."

Finally one day when he said that, I asked, "What circumstances?" He was startled and a bit embarrassed, and it took him a moment to realize that I was responding to what he had just said.

"Ah, well, that's just an expression," he said somewhat defensively. Then after some reflection, he added, "It's true nonetheless, isn't it? Life does have a way of kickin' the joy out of us, doesn't it?"

The man's candor was quite representative of the many questions and comments that come to me. Not long ago someone wrote and asked, "How can you keep a joyous attitude when life wears you down? What do you do when life seems to go stale with sameness?"

Another person wrote, "I hear a lot about the fact that Christians should always be joyous. I believe in Christ, but it's difficult to be joyful all the time, especially when I have to work with non-Christians who make it difficult to be positive about life."

Someone else confessed, "The joy I felt when I became a Christian seems to have drained away. Life has settled back into the same dull round of responsibilities, and I don't feel much different than before I was a Christian."

And finally, an exceptionally honest person put it this way, "I'm really concerned about the joyless example I am to my family and friends. Circumstances and situations get me down and it's difficult to feel consistently joyous. We're not expected to feel joy all the time are we? Hope not, because I sure don't!"

Does any of this sound familiar? Was the shopkeeper in Edinburgh right? Can life kick the joy out of us? Can we be only as joyful as the circumstances in which we find ourselves allow? Is joy dependent on things going our way, on people's attitudes, on good health and pleasant surroundings?

No, I don't believe that for a minute in spite of the heading of this chapter. I purposely worded it that way so I could contradict it for emphasis. Life can't kick the joy out of us—not authentic joy and it is that I want to look closely at now.

There's a delightful story told about Lloyd Douglas, author of *The Robe*. He enjoyed visiting a little old violin teacher in a shabby, small walk-up room he proudly called his studio.

Douglas liked to drop in on him because he had the kind of lovely wisdom about life that refreshed him. One morning, he stopped by to see the old man. "Well what's the good news today?" he asked. Putting down his violin, he stepped over to a tuning fork suspended from a silk cord. He struck it a smart blow with a padded mallet and said, "There's the good news for today. That, my friend, is 'A.' It was 'A' all day yesterday. It will be 'A' all day tomorrow, next week, and for a thousand years."

That story tunes our minds to the "A" of true joy. Like Christ, who is its only source, joy is the same yesterday, today, and tomorrow. It is artesian, never changes, and is consistent irrespective of people or circumstances. At the same time, joy is not a quality we can find by searching or earn by effort. It comes from something—really Someone else.

True Joy

Here are some basic thoughts to guide our thinking concerning true joy.

1. Joy resounds in the heart of God and is an outward expression of His love.

2. Joy is the ecstasy of heaven and the triumphant experience of those who have begun eternal life here and now.

3. Joy was revealed in Jesus Christ, the joyous heart of God with us. Everything He said and did for us—His life, message, death, resurrection, and the gift of His Spirit at Pentecost—was so we could have lasting joy.

4. Joy can be our consistent experience by abiding in Christ's love and allowing Him to abide in us.

5. Joy is the identifiable mark of a Christian and a truly vital church. A joyless Christian is a contradiction of terms.

6. Joy is not an option. The inalienable right of the people of our lives is that we should radiate, model, and communicate consistent joy.

You may have cheered with affirmation as you read the first four of the above presuppositions. Did the last two give you pause? Did you want to say, "Hold on! Isn't that expecting too much?" Before I answer, let me reflect briefly on what Jesus had to say about this joy which He offers to us.

Jesus' Promise of Joy

In the Lord's farewell conversation with His disciples on the night before He was crucified, He reemphasized His teaching with these words. "These things I have spoken to you, that My joy may remain in you, and that your joy may be full" (John 15:11). The words leap off the page. My joy! Remaining joy! . . . Full joy! . . . not in part, but overflowing!

As we reflect on what Jesus said there we can't help but take a closer look at the first ten verses to learn what He meant by "these things." But before we can fully appreciate the impact of what He had said, we need to understand the setting in which He said them.

Joy in the True Vine

The fourteenth chapter of John ends with Jesus saying, ". . . Arise, let us go from here" (John 14:31). That means that Jesus and the disciples left the Upper Room and moved through Jerusalem toward the Garden of Gethsemane. I think the rest of Jesus' farewell discourse, recorded in John 15 and 16, may have been given while passing through the city, pausing along the way for intense conversation. When He had finished teaching He then prayed the prayer recorded in John 17. After that He and the disciples went out of the city and on to Gethsemane.

On the way, it is very likely that they would have paused at the Temple. Over the principal gate of the Temple was a magnificently carved golden vine symbolic of Israel as the vine of God from the times the prophets of Israel had taken great pride in its calling to be the "vine of the Lord." The Psalmist expresses this in his prayer to God in Psalm 80:8–9: "You have brought a vine out of Egypt; you have cast out the nations and planted it. You prepared room for it and caused it to take deep root. . . ." Isaiah claims the same assurance, "the vineyard of the Lord of hosts is the house of Israel. . ." (Isa. 5:7). And Jeremiah quotes the Lord's reminder that Israel is His "noble vine" (Jer. 2:21). I think it is quite likely that it was beneath the golden vine over the Temple gate that

Jesus gave the parable of the vine and the branches. In that context Jesus' words "I am the true vine" take an even deeper meaning. He, not Israel, was the true vine of God.

The actual meaning of Jesus' I AM assertion is, "I am the vine, the true." In so stating, He establishes not only His authority, but His authenticity. He marks the beginning of a new age. No longer is Israel, or tradition, or heritage, or nationality the source of receiving God's blessing, but now that blessing is given in and through Him, the divine Mediator. You and I are invited to live in this new age receiving the unlimited blessings He offers us.

Following this bold claim Jesus gives the parable of the vine and the branches. In it He reminds the disciples—and us— of the interdependence of the vine and the branches in produc- ing fruit. The purpose of the vine is to give life-giving sap to the branches and the purpose of the branches is to bear fruit. When the branches bear fruit, they are pruned back so that in the next season they will bring forth even more fruit. But those that do not bear fruit are cut off entirely, and thrown away.

Then with unmistakable impact, Jesus draws the incisive implications of His parable for His relationship with us, "Abide in Me, and I in you. As the branch cannot bear fruit of itself, unless it abides in the vine, neither can you, unless you abide in Me. I am the vine, you are the branches. He who abides in Me, and I in him, bears much fruit; for without Me you can do nothing" (John 15:4–5).

The purpose of the parable of the vine and the branches in the light of Jesus' statement, "These things I have spoken to you, that My joy may remain in you. . ." (John 15:11) is to vividly portray the source of joy, the satisfaction of joy, the secret of receiving and maintaining lasting joy, the signifi- cance of joy in Christ's strategy for reaching the world, and the strength of joy in our problems. Taken in that order, we'll discover a joy that life can't kick out of us.

Jesus Is Joy

Christ Himself is the source of joy. The sap of the vine which surges into the branches is grace—unqualified love. The words grace and joy come from the same Greek root. Joy is the delight of being loved. Everything that Christ said and did and continues to do in our lives today tells us that we are cherished, valued, and loved. He died for us, rose from the dead for us, and is with us now, and is ready to heal us with accepting and affirming love.

There is no authentic joy apart from being loved by Christ. His joy persists regardless of life's circumstances. On the other hand, happiness is conditioned by what's happening to and around us. The word "happiness" comes from "hap," chance. And chances change. That's why there is such a great difference between happiness and joy. Life is undependable; human affection is often conditioned by our adequacy or performance and situations we counted on remaining stable can fluctuate and scuttle our carefully laid plans.

Whenever our security is in people or possessions, we may know a measure of happiness for a time, but not joy. That precious spiritual gift is the result of experiencing a love that will never change, that not even our failures will diminish in the least degree and that will remain constant whatever people do or say to hurt us. Where do you find a love like that? Only in Christ. And from that gracious love joy flows.

Joy Is Knowing We're Accepted

Joy is profound acceptance. You may react to the use of the word acceptance. Doesn't that result in being falsely content with the way we are? Isn't there a chance that we'll stop trying to grow and improve? No. One of the most exciting discoveries I've made is that creative efforts to be all that Christ means us to be emerge out of a deep sense that He is pleased with us. Nothing robs us of joy as much as the nagging feeling of not measuring up, of having to do something to gain approval.

In human relations in the family, at work, and among our friends so often the reward system is used to instigate change or improvement of behavior. We withhold affection or acceptance until people do what we want. That creates the tension of insecurity of never quite knowing how we stand. When love is freely given, we have the will to press on to our next stage of growth. We all know our faults and areas in which we need to change. Lasting character development happens in the context of grace, not judgment. When we know someone really loves us and cares about us, we are free to talk about our weaknesses and do something about them. The judgment of Christ is always coupled with His grace.

A young pastor friend of mine is discovering this. He was raised in a family in which qualified love and approval pervaded his home. His parents were stingy affirmers. They feared that praise and approbation would lead to pride and self-satisfaction in their son. He grew up with the inner insecurity of not measuring up. In his teens, he made a commitment to Christ, but somehow missed His grace. His desire to "measure up" was transferred to Christ. All through college and seminary he worked hard and earned good grades, not because he knew he was loved by the Lord but in an effort to earn His love.

When my friend was called to become the pastor of a church, he turned into a kind of "super parent" for his congregation. He preached judgment, the need for repentance and gathered a growing congregation of people who needed to be told how bad they were and gladly accepted his clearly defined rules and regulations of how to be obedient followers of Christ. Judgmentalism within the congregation and toward outsiders became the spirit dominating the life of the young pastor's church. Since many people need that brand of rigidity, the church continued to grow with new members who enjoyed being scolded in the sermon and feeling guilty as the basis of trying to improve. Because of the growth of his church, the pastor thought he was a success.

I met this rigid young man at a conference. His facial expressions and body language exposed his tightly bound-up personality. I soon discovered that he was not really listening to my messages, but was checking them out for his brand of orthodoxy. He found my theme that week—freedom in Christ—very threatening.

One evening my sermon centered on the grace and joy of the cross. I simply explained what it means to accept and live by grace and the contagious joy that results. The Spirit of Christ moved mightily in my friend's mind. The illustrations I gave of people whose experience of grace had made them truly joyous convinced him that joy was the missing ingredient in his life and ministry. At the conclusion of my message I asked people to find one other person in their small groups to reflect on what I'd said, and pray for each other. The man singled me out to be his partner. I was both amazed and thankful for what he shared with me.

"Tonight," he said, "I realized that I've never really felt loved or accepted just as I am. I've been afraid to preach grace because I felt it would lead people into careless complacency or undisciplined living. I guess I've feared what I'd do myself if I dared to believe that the Lord accepts me as I am. Inside, I've felt like an over-wound-up spring. And yet, in the meeting tonight, I felt like I was being bathed with grace. I could not stop it and didn't want to. It's as if I've come to the cross for the first time. I feel forgiven, loved, and free. The Lord reached inside me and sprung that tightly wound spring. I still feel it unwinding inside me. I never realized how tense I'd become." We talked and prayed late into the night, sharing our mutual joy.

The young man returned to his church a very different person. He was no less committed to biblical preaching or to teaching the doctrines of the faith, but his new-found grace and joy brought a fresh power to his ministry. We visit often in letters or over the phone. He's pressing on in his growth in Christ and helping set his people free. He has discovered that there is no limit to what can happen when grace is the motivation and joy is the quality of a congregation's life. He no longer uses negative criticism and judgmentalism as a manipulative tool to keep people in line or force their involvement. I've told this man's story with his permission and encouragement. He wants everyone to find the joy he's experiencing.

One of the most exciting things I observe happening in America today is the renewal I see sweeping across the land. It's happening to Christians who have received fresh grace for their deepest needs and as a result are exuding a joy which radiates in their lives.

The Secret of Lasting Joy

But can that quality of joy be maintained? Does it last? Not unless we discover Jesus' secret of full, artesian joy. He said, "Abide in Me, and I in you." The vital connection of the vine and the branch is the secret. If joy is the outward expression of the inner experience of grace, it follows naturally that a daily, hourly replenishment of grace is the only way to maintain our joy.

The verb "abide" in Greek is *menō*. It means "to take up permanent residence, to settle in, rest." To abide in Christ means to stop trying to earn His acceptance or to work to justify our right to be His person. We are to relax and receive His grace. That becomes very practical in dealing with our problems. Each day's problems become opportunities to trust Him and receive renewed grace. We do not need to be strong, clever, or resourceful to abide. Instead, we are to abandon ourselves to Him, trusting Him with our problems, and accept His assurance that He will assume responsibility for us and our problems.

I like the way J. C. Ryle interpreted the meaning of Jesus'

command to abide in Him: "Abide in Me. Cling to Me. Stick fast to Me. Live the life of close and intimate communion with Me. Get nearer and nearer to Me. Roll every burden on Me. Cast your whole weight on Me. Never let go your hold on Me for a moment. Be as it were rooted and planted in Me. Do this, and I will never fail you." *

The other half of the secret of lasting joy is that Christ abides—lives—in us. He gives us exactly what we need in any moment: assurance that we are loved in our problems, forgiveness for our mistakes, wisdom to discern what He wants to do to bring good out of difficulties, and supernatural strength to do what He guides in untangling our problems. There is no joy when we are worried about whether we'll have what it takes. But equally so, there is no joy to be compared to the joy we feel when we know that we are empowered by the Savior of the world! That means accepting His strength pulsing into us as branches inseparably connected to Him, the vine.

Christ's Daring Strategy

Why is Christ willing to love and bless and empower us as His branches? Because there is nothing more magnetic and attractive in a Christian than vibrant joy. When people see and feel it in us they want to know how they can find it for themselves. We are essential in Christ's strategy for reaching the people around us. That's what is behind the daring allegory of the mutual dependence of the vine and the branches. The branches cannot produce fruit without the vine. "For without Me you can do nothing." But don't miss the other side of that truth. The vine cannot produce fruit without the branches!

Jesus shows us that not only do we need Him but, by divine

---

* John Ryle, *Expository Thoughts on the Gospels*, vol. 4 (Grand Rapids: Baker Book House, 1977).

condescension, He needs us and has chosen to use us in reaching others. It was as if He said, "Apart from Me you can do nothing, and according to the strategy for reaching the world I have adopted, apart from you I will do nothing." Of course, Christ can do anything He wants. He is all-powerful. But for the spreading of His gospel of grace and exemplifying the joy He wants for everyone, He has chosen to work through human agents like you and me! And the way He's selected to do it is to meet our needs with His all-sufficient love so that we, as branches, will produce the fruit of joy. He knows that our joy will be irresistible and will draw people to us so that we can share with them the source of that joy in His grace.

That's why the Master put such an emphasis on joy when He talked to His disciples that night. He wanted His joy to be the undeniable characteristic of His followers and of the church He would establish through them. His presence in them and with them would be the reason for that joy. He went to the cross to provide an endless flow of the grace which would nourish that joy. When He arose from the dead, His first word to His followers was "Joy!" And later, when He filled His disciples with His Spirit at Pentecost, joy pulsated in their lives and became the quality that attracted others to the group of Christians. At any really vital and productive period of growth and expansion of the church through history, two ingredients have been present: profound grace and exuberant joy.

A Commitment to Joyous Living

As I have reflected on the thought that joy is Christ's strategy for reaching others through us, the question has arisen in my mind—"Do I express that kind of joy in my words and actions? Is joy a word people would use to describe my attitude, especially in the problems and pressures of life?"

These questions have then caused me to ask myself why

at certain times do I communicate anything less than joy? Usually it's because I have taken my eyes off of Christ and fastened them on difficult circumstances. A lack of joy usually alerts me to the fact that I've cut off the flow of grace by trying too hard through self-effort. Most of all, times of joylessness have alarmed me with the realization that in a busy life I have not taken time to "abide in the vine" and allow Him to infuse His gracious Spirit and healing love into me as His branch.

Daily prayer and Bible study can become routine and ineffective unless they are "abiding times" of resting in Christ's presence, letting go of our tight grip of worry over problems, and allowing Him to love us. At moments like this, He will help us to visualize, actually see, ourselves as joyous people able to cope with the problems ahead of us. The amazing thing to me is that the picture comes true!

Joy is not an option. It's what the Lord desires and what the world around us desperately needs. The joy of being loved is inseparable from the joy of loving.

Sharing the Joy of Heaven—Now!

Allowing the Lord's grace to produce the fruit of joy in us gives us an opportunity to participate in the joy of heaven. There's great joy in heaven whenever people receive God's grace. The parables of the lost sheep, the lost coin, and the lost son in Luke fifteen sound this recurring theme. When the shepherd finds his lost sheep, he exclaims with joy, ". . . Rejoice with me, for I have found my sheep which was lost!" And Jesus underlines the meaning. "I say to you that likewise there will be more joy in heaven over one sinner who repents than over ninety-nine just persons who need no repentance" (Luke 15:6–7).

The same joy is reiterated in the parable of the woman who lost one of the ten silver coins from her precious necklace. We can understand her feelings when we recall the tradition that necklaces of coins were given as a wedding gift by a groom to his bride. No wonder she searched so diligently for the one coin that was lost from her necklace. And when she found it, she wanted all of her friends and neighbors to share her joy. Again Jesus emphasizes the meaning. "Likewise, I say to you, there is joy in the presence of the angels of God over one sinner who repents" (Luke 15:10).

Then to drive home the point in the most personal way, Jesus told the parable of the lost son and the joy of his father at his return. Note the progression: joy in heaven, joy among the angels of God, and then the joy of a father. And we know the father in the story is none other than our heavenly Father. It's very moving to know that you and I can be the cause of a celebration in heaven. It happened when we first accepted grace and is continued as we abide in Christ more deeply and express His joy.

But more than that, we can join in the celebration. As we become concerned about people and care about their deep need to know Christ and His unqualified love for them, we will be given opportunities to share our faith. And when we help them turn their lives over to Christ's management, we will know the sublime joy of helping them live forever. There's no lasting joy without that quality of involvement in helping people meet Christ and learn how to abide in Him. Our joy is multiplied when we share their newfound joy.

The lack of vibrant joy in so many Christians today may be explained by the neglect of this central calling of every follower of Christ. The initial joy we knew when we became Christians is soon lost if we keep it to ourselves. And that's tragic with so many people around us who are longing to find joy.

Joy in Our Problems

But that leads to a question I hear often these days. "How can I be a good witness and communicate my faith if I still have problems?" If we wait until we have a problem-free life in order to feel that we are adequate examples of new life in Christ, we will never get around to sharing our faith. I know so many Christians who think that they must have life together in every area before they can be effective witnesses. That's preposterous—who ever reaches that point?

It's the joy we show in the midst of life's difficulties and problems that will be attractive to others. Our impelling witness will be of how joy can be realized while we are growing through the very problems we are facing. What people most need to see is what Nehemiah reminded the people of Israel, ". . . the joy of the Lord is your strength" (Neh. 8:10).

The Pruning Through Problems

That brings me to a final thought. I have kept an aspect of Jesus' parable of the vine and the branches to highlight that a crucial part of being a fruit-bearing branch of Christ is to be pruned. "Every branch in Me that does not bear fruit He takes away; and every branch that bears fruit He prunes, that it may bear more fruit" (John 15:2). Pruning of the vine is to cut back so that the sap does not uselessly run out into unproductive, trailing branches on which no fruit can grow. The pruning process centers the flow of the sap for the one purpose for which the branch exists—to produce fruit. It seems like a painful process but the subsequent fruitage is worth it.

Problems, when surrendered to the Lord, do to us what pruning does to a branch. They focus us back on the vine and His resources of grace to strengthen us. And it's usually after trusting the Lord with a problem and experiencing His help to conquer it, that we know greater joy than before. So a vital key to a joy-filled life is accepting the problems and allowing the Lord to use them to focus the flow of His divine energy into us.

Often the branch of our busy life grows off in all directions.

We become so over-involved in our own activities that some of the off-shoots of our branch forget that they are attached to the vine. At times, our problems alert us to the fact that we've tried to live without Christ's grace and power. Then the crisis prunes us back to Him and His plan and purpose for us. Uncreative activities, eccentric behavior, distracting thoughts the Lord can't bless, and frantic busyness are pruned and we can get back to our central purpose of living by grace, modeling joy, and loving people. The Lord cares for us so much He will prune anything that robs us of joy. When we abide in Him, nothing or no one, not even life itself, can kick the joy out of us!

> God is a zealous pruner,
> For He knows—
> Who, falsely tender, spares the knife
> But spoils the rose.*

---

* John Oxenham. 1852–1941. By permission of Desmond Dunkerley.

13

PEOPLE
PROBLEMS

THE WELL-SCRUBBED BOY sat with his parents in the front pew during my closing sermon at a preaching mission in a church in Southern California. Not once did he take his eyes off of me. I was immensely encouraged by his attention.

My theme that night was centered on the idea that we are called not only to be Christ's friends, but in turn to be friends to others in His name. And my special application called for us to be friends even to those who have hurt, disappointed, or frustrated us.

At the conclusion of my sermon, I gave an invitation for people to come forward to pray for the healing of memories and for the courage to be initiative agents of healing to people who distressed them. No one moved, and the minutes ticked by in an uncomfortable silence.

Suddenly, the boy in the front row jumped to his feet. His mother, realizing that he might be responding to the invitation, reached out and grabbed hold of his jacket. But he was determined and moved out into the aisle and almost ran to where I was standing, and knelt.

Placing my hands on the boy's shoulders I asked, "What do you want me to pray about?" He looked up into my eyes and said, "A couple of my friends have really been mean and hard on me. Please ask Jesus to help me be the kind of friend to them I wish they'd be to me."

I was deeply moved as I prayed that the boy would accept Jesus' friendship and have the courage to be His friend to his buddies who were troubling him. During my prayer, I choked up with emotion and tears streamed down my face.

When I finished, the boy looked up into my face. "Why are you crying, Dr. Ogilvie?" he asked with concern and wonderment.

"That's the prayer I most need to pray too. Some of my friends have hurt me, and you've shown me that I need to forgive them and be their friend regardless of what they have done."

"Wow!" the boy exclaimed. "You'd better kneel down and ask Jesus to help you!" With that he smiled and returned to his parents who were anxiously waiting for him in the front pew.

He was right. So I walked around the kneeling rail, threw a quick glance of appeal for help to one of the pastors of the church, and knelt for prayer. The sensitive pastor moved out of his place, down to where I was kneeling, received my confession and desire to be healed, and laid his hands on me and prayed. When he finished, I returned to my place behind the rail and repeated the invitation, after sharing honestly what had just happened to me.

That broke open the floodgate of the Lord's power. Hundreds of people came forward for prayer that night. The Lord had used a young boy to touch the hearts of both the visiting preacher and the people. "Out of the mouths of babes . . ." or young people, or any vulnerable person, the Lord seeks to break through with healing.

I've shared this personal story as my own witness of how we all need Christ's healing of our hurts over what people do and say. He showed me what I needed to do about three specific people in my own life. These were some friends whose attitudes and words had cut me deeply. One was trying to hurt me, the second was hurting someone I love, and the third was hurting himself. We all have people like that. We can more easily shake off the criticism or gossip of a disturbed person who feels called to straighten us out than we can the pain someone causes people we love. And perhaps most distressing of all is watching a person on a no-win course heading for disaster.

Before that night these people caused me a combination of frustration, indignation, and worry. But the Lord knew my need and got to me through the honesty and winsome directness of a young boy. After receiving healing, I said to myself, "I can't wait to see these people and tell them of my love and friendship."

Do you identify with what I shared? Can you empathize from your own experience with the challenge to be a friend even though some people act in very unfriendly ways?

Let's face it—so many of our problems are caused by "people"—people who are difficult to love, people whose personalities grate on us, people who misuse and take advantage of us. And added to that list are people who call themselves our friends and yet stand in the way of our progress, people who hurt those we love, and people whose selfishness makes a relationship with them an endurance contest.

Christ comes to us in many ways—through prayer and reading the Bible; He speaks through the world around us and within us as the inner voice of guidance and assurance. He also speaks to us through our friends. How thankful we should be for friends who have prayed for us, affirmed us, cheered our efforts, and stood by us in times of failure or discouragement.

But I believe the Lord also comes to us in the difficult problem people of our lives. He told us that what we do for the hungry, the thirsty, the stranger, the naked and sick, the imprisoned, we do for Him: "Inasmuch as you did it to one of the least of these My brethren, you did it to Me" (Matt. 25:40). Could not the same be true of the people who trouble us? Have you ever stopped to think that how we respond to the needs of problem people may be our response to Christ? Browning's caution may well apply here, "Hush, I pray you! What if this friend happens to be God?"

I'm sure we all long for the Spirit of Christ to dwell in us and empower us for life's challenges. It may be that sometimes He answers that longing by sending people whose problems cause us problems. When that happens, we are reminded of just how much we need Him. He has allowed their problems to become our concern because He wants to use us in His healing ministry in their lives. For that ministry He offers us a great promise.

A Promise for People Problems

Jesus' promise for problem people is given us as a further explanation of the parable of the vine and the branches that we looked at earlier. The sap of the vine which surges into us as branches is not only Christ's unqualified love for us, but is meant to produce the fruit of friendship and love to others. In John 15:12–17, Jesus promises to be our Friend and make us friends in His name to the very people who often least deserve it.

What an exciting and yet down to earth way to look at the Christian life! We are friends of Christ by His choice. That should give our self-esteem a boost. But also, we are called to be to others the kind of friend He is to us. He is consistent, faithful, forgiving, caring, and not put off by the things we do or say. We are to think of our ministry as His followers as a profound expression of His absolutely reliable and self-giving example of true friendship.

It is fascinating to note that God established both the old and the new covenants with the bond of friendship. He called Abraham and promised him friendship. The patriarch was called a "friend of God." And Moses, to whom He gave the Commandments of that covenant, "Spoke to God as a man to his friend." The heroes and heroines of the Old Testament did the magnificent, impossibility-defying things they did because of their close friendship with God that in no way negated their awe and reverence for Him.

And now here is Christ, "the Messenger of the covenant" as He was identified by Malachi (Mal. 3:1) saying, "I have called you [My] friends . . ." (John 15:15). In a sublime way, He was a Friend in search of friends with whom He could establish the new Israel, the church, and through whom His strategy of reconciling the world to Himself would be exemplified and spread abroad in the world.

Is the word friendship too insignificant a designation for our relationship with Christ? Is it too subjective to say with the hymn writer James Small, "I found a Friend, O such a Friend, He loved me ere I knew Him"? I don't think so.

I remember overhearing two of the world's greatest preachers talking at a conference in Switzerland about what they were to preach about the following Sunday. One of them said he was going to preach about friendship with Christ. The other preacher commented, "That's a rather lightweight topic, isn't it?" His friend replied pointedly, "Only if you have a lightweight idea of the meaning of friendship!"

For Christ, friendship with His followers was anything but lightweight or sentimental. In fact, in the Savior we experience a quality of friendship which elevates and enlarges our definition of what it means to be a friend. From the Master we discover what friendship really is, the lengths to which it goes in expression of loyal love, and the healing results it has in filling the "Friend-shaped" emptiness in all of us.

The promise that Christ is our friend and that He calls us to be His friends is nestled between two commands in John 15:12–17 which prepare us for His friendship, and two assurances which spell out its implications. And as we shall see, Jesus gives us an awesome command and a costly condition, and then He offers us the enabling connection with Him in the "vine-branches" quality of friendship. That is followed by an undeniable call to action and a liberating kind of confidence to live out that calling. Let's look at these five aspects of being a friend and having friends that are found in these verses.

The Awesome Command

We can imagine how startled the disciples were when Jesus said, "This is My commandment, that you love one another as I have loved you" (John 15:12). They had known Christ's love as they had walked with Him along the dusty roads of Palestine. He had loved them by seeing their potential and by forgiving their mistakes and their slowness to understand.

The disciples had felt the Lord's tender care and faithful concern for them. And now He called them to love others as He had loved them. Out ahead they would understand the depth of Christ's love when they looked back at the cross. But at this point their understanding of His command to love as He had loved them was wrapped up in all they had seen and heard during the three years of their life together. During that time He never gave up on them even though they often resisted His message, went against His purposes, and squabbled with each other over prestige.

We learn from this how we are to look at the people in our lives who disappoint or trouble us. Loving others as Christ has loved us lifts our relationships above the bartered quality of love. When we think of how relentless He has been in caring for us when we have resisted His friendship, we begin to understand in a small way the kind of friend He wants us to be to others.

So often, it is selfishness that turns others, and us, into being problem people. When we focus only on what *we* want or what *we* need, we are insensitive to the effect we are having on other people. Then, too, there's an interesting principle that goes on—what we consider a problem in others is often a problem in us. And when we complain to the Lord about the way we are treated, His response is, "I'm surprised you are surprised. I meet the same willfulness in you. And I've never given up on you!"

And so we begin in our consideration of what it means to be a friend by really taking seriously this awesome command to love as Christ has loved us. That's very challenging. For starters that means that our love is never dependent on the performance or consistency of the people we are called by the Lord to befriend. If our expression of friendship is qualified by people measuring up, then we are still bound up in our own brand of selfishness. To break that bind we need the next aspect of Christ's call to befriend others in His name.

The Costly Condition

The cure for selfishness is self-sacrifice. The Master follows His commandment to love as He has loved by telling us about the high cost of that love. "Greater love has no one than this, than to lay down one's life for his friends" (John 15:13). The example of *how* Christ had loved them is now expanded to include the *way* He would love them. By implication, both are included in His commandment to love as He loves. In trying to understand what is meant by that, it will be helpful to ask what laying down His life meant for Christ, what it meant to the disciples, and what it means for us today.

In Christ's story about His ministry as the Good Shepherd, He says that He lays down His life for the sheep. The image is filled with tender care and protection. In watching over sheep, a shepherd would call them into the sheepfold at night and then would lie down across the entrance. Actually, he would be the door. The sheep couldn't wander out into danger and hungry wolves couldn't get in to harm them.

But Jesus had more than protection in mind in His metaphor. For Him, laying down His life meant the cross. "Therefore

My Father loves Me, because I lay down My life that I may take it again. No one takes it from Me, but I lay it down of Myself. I have power to lay it down, and I have power to take it again. This command I have received from My Father" (John 10:17–18). Calvary would be the place where He would lay down His life, and the empty tomb and His resurrected presence would be the evidence that He had taken it up again in victory.

To lay down one's life meant death. The disciples understood that. This is what Peter had meant earlier in the Upper Room—he would lay down his life for the Master. But the Lord put this boast of faithfulness into a realistic perspective when He said, "Will you lay down your life for My sake? Most assuredly, I say to you, the rooster shall not crow till you have denied Me three times" (John 13:38). In substance, Jesus was saying, "Will you die for Me? Be careful about such offers of self-sacrifice. My friend, you won't even make it through tonight without denying Me to save your own skin!"

Jesus knew that Peter would deny Him and some of the other disciples would desert Him during the crucifixion. But He also knew that His laying down His life on the cross would be an unforgettable expression of His friendship for them. More than that, they would come to believe that His cross had been a complete forgiveness of their sins and the establishment of their eternal reconciliation with God. That unqualified grace would become the motivation of the self-sacrificing love of the disciples for each other and for the world.

And it happened. When Christ returned after the resurrection and ascension, He filled the disciples with His Spirit. They were known for the friendship they shared with Him and each other. That friendship spilled over to others and the circle of their Christ-centered friendship widened to include all classes of people from all races whom the disciples won to Christ through their contagious love, and their straightforward preaching and sacrificial giving of themselves and their possessions. John explains the reason for their remarkable success. "By this we know love, because He laid down His life for us. And we also ought to lay down our lives for the brethren" (1 John 3:16).

For some of the disciples, the costly condition of laying down their lives led to martyrdom. They died for their faith and their love for Christ and one another. That causes us to wonder what laying down our lives for our friends means for us today.

In our relationships, laying down our lives and taking up our daily cross means sacrificing ourselves for others. Sacrifice? Let the word stand. It means our offering of ourselves in costly service for others. Spelled out in practicalities, it means putting the needs of others before our own comfort and pleasure.

That makes the cost of loving very high. It means both vulnerability and viability. We must be willing to surrender our privacy, time, energy, and money, and be open to give away all that we are and have to others. It means forgiving even before people ask to be forgiven. We must pray to discover what love requires in each relationship, even with people who find it difficult to ask for help.

In laying down our lives, the ball is always in our court. We're called to take the initiative, to take the first step.

The Enabling Connection

We cannot respond to the high cost of loving without the daily experience of what I like to call the enabling connection of the vine and the branch. In John 15:14 Jesus says, "You are My friends if you do whatever I command you." The source of the love we need to express is the sap of His Spirit moving from Him, the vine, into us, the branches. It is through this love-connection that we listen for the Lord's guidance for what He wants us to say and do. What a great promise! We will be given orders for what it will mean to be Christ's love to people. When we ask, He will make it plain. Be sure of that! But also be sure of something else: When we do today what He tells us to do in our problematical relationships, we will receive further clarity in the future. The Lord draws us into His confidence, helps us to picture what we are to express, and then promises to be with us to give us the strength to implement that guidance.

This is the cooperative partnership we are offered in Christ's promise that He is our Friend and we are called to be His friends. And so He goes on to affirm, "No longer do I call you servants, for a servant does not know what his master is doing; but I have called you friends, for all things that I heard from My Father I have made known to you" (v. 15).

We are profoundly moved by the trust our Friend places in us as His friends. No longer are we only servants with the mandate, "Ours is not to question why, but to do with no reply," but now we are friends with the motto, "Ours is to know the reason why and to do is our reply." We are given the mind of Christ to understand, the grace of Christ to express His love, the power of the indwelling Christ to act in the most creative way, and at the right time.

One of my favorite passages of Scripture, Ephesians 3:17–21, underlines Jesus' promise to be our Friend and what is available to us through that friendship. Paul prays for the Ephesian Christians, "that Christ may dwell in your hearts through faith; that you, being rooted and grounded in love, may be able to comprehend with all the saints what is the width and length and depth and height—*to know the love of Christ which passes knowledge;* that you may be filled with all the fullness of God. Now to Him who is able to do exceedingly abundantly above all that we ask or think, according to the power that works in us, to Him be glory in the church by Christ Jesus throughout all ages, world without end. Amen" (italics mine).

All that is offered to us when we become involved with Christ in reaching out to the problem-people in our lives. Our reach will widen to surround them with acceptance, it will be unlimited in the lengths to which it will reach in

forgiveness, it will be inexhaustible in the depth of its resource-
fulness, and it will have no cap on the height of its expectation.
The Lord wants us to experience the enabling power of the
fullness of His indwelling love. As the Vine, His love surges
through us in abundance. And that changes our attitude toward the very people who have stretched our patience or
caused us pain. The Lord is ready to stretch our imaginations
to the possibilities for these people—beyond what we would
"ask or think."

George Whitefield, the great preacher and evangelist, once
was asked, "Do you ever tire of your work for the Lord?"
He answered, "Sometimes I tire in it, but never of it." We've
all known times when being an initiative friend—reaching
out, forgiving, caring, giving, listening—has been depleting.
But when, like Whitefield, we maintain the enabling connection, we are given fresh energy and willingness when we need
it most. That replenishment is given through the next aspect
of Christ's friendship.

An Undeniable Call

There's a great freedom in knowing that we are chosen and
appointed by Christ to be His friends and that we are to befriend others, even the most difficult people in our lives. Jesus
said "You did not choose Me, but I chose you and appointed
you that you should go and bear fruit, and that your fruit
should remain . . ." (John 15:16).

Our fruit-bearing ministry as friends of the Lord is His idea.
He has called us to it. Here's a purpose big enough to make
life exciting. And do we have to question our authority? He
is the prime mover—always ahead of us and always anticipating our needs. He chose us, called us, and we can be sure
that He goes before us to prepare the way for our efforts to
befriend others.

The late Lillian Dickson, leader of the Mustard Seed Mission, used to say, "The knowledge of the need is a call of
God." When we become aware of a need in another person's

life, it is never a question of what the Lord will do, but of what *we* are willing to allow Him to do through us.

This ties in with the central idea of this whole book: When the Lord allows a big problem to surface, it is because He is ready to do a great work. And we are called to be His agents of healing, His workers. As we work for Him, we will learn to look at the problems people are wrestling with as the opportunity for them to either meet their Friend, Jesus Christ, or be drawn into deeper, intimate relationship with Him.

Presenting Christ as Friend and the Christian life as friendship with Him is the most effective means of fruit-bearing evangelism. The test of our friendship with Christ is that we introduce others to Him as life's greatest Friend. All of His love, atoning death, resurrection power, and abiding presence can be summarized in this lovely word "Friend." Jesus is the friend of sinners—the lonely, the insecure, the troubled. And when we listen to them with empathy and sensitivity, we will have earned the right and have the credibility to tell them what our Friend has done for us and is ready to do for them.

Some of the most effective, reproductive, fruit-bearing Christians I know think of their efforts to win others to Christ as the awesome privilege of simply being friends. And their caring and concern for people is not resisted as religious zeal or manipulation.

As a friend of mine says, "I just make as many deep friendships with people as I can. Then when life perks some big problem to the surface in their lives, I'm ready and available to stand with them. And somewhere along the way I get my chance to share what my Friend Christ can make out of the raw material of problems." Dozens of people have become alive in Christ and will live forever because of his friendship evangelism. His fruit remains . . . it lasts.

The idea of friendship evangelism can change our attitude toward problem people. Instead of being obstructions to our plans or happiness they become opportunities.

This simply means that when this kind of person disturbs

us it is time to ask, "Lord, what's Your plan and strategy? Change my attitude, give me Your love and patience. I surrender to You anything that is contributing to a negative picture of this person. Help me Lord. I can't do it by myself with all my judgments and lack of faith, but You can do something wonderful in this person's life."

So often, though, we hesitate to befriend problem-people because of the false notion that our gesture of friendship will in some way look like we are condoning their actions and patterns of behavior. Actually, just the opposite usually happens. It is in an environment of friendship—Christ-inspired and -guided friendship—that people change. Blasting a person with advice never works. Blaming is not our business; providing the friendly relationships in which people can share and face their problems is our calling.

A Liberating Confidence

We are not left without help in the pursuit of our calling. Christ concludes this part of His farewell message to the disciples—and us—by assuring us that, "Whatever you ask from My Father in My name He may give you."

There are two assurances we need in our ministry of befriending others, particularly problem-people. We need to know that human nature can be changed by Christ and that our intercessory prayers are answered when we ask for that miracle.

We live in a time that questions both of these assurances. Many, some of them Christians, believe that human nature is the unchangeable result of environment and conditioning. Therefore, they say, we must remain what our formative years have made us. To be sure, some admit that minor adjustments can be made and some attitudes can be altered. But there is little support for the conviction that our basic nature can be transformed. Amazing, that in our age of technological advancement, computers, and space travel, we find it so difficult to believe in the possibility of character transformation.

The reason for this is that many scientists base their confidence on human skill and many church leaders think that the time of Christ's miracles was confined to His incarnate ministry and the Apostolic Age.

I, for one, am convinced that now is a very special time in history in which Christ is very active performing miracles—physically, psychologically, and spiritually. And prayer in His name releases His healing power.

Satan has perpetrated a lie and so many Christians have accepted it as inevitable truth. It's that Christ's Spirit at work in a person cannot change his or her basic nature and personality structure. As a result, most churches think their only calling is to help people believe in Christ and then to help them experience His comfort in coping with the difficulties of living with the person life has made them and the troubled world as it is. The church becomes a hand-holding support fellowship to help us make it from week to week. We expect little ever to change in people's make-up and that's what we get . . . very little!

All that I've said so far in this chapter about being loving, affirming, forgiving, and supportive friends is urgently needed for our relationships. But I can't end there. Christ didn't. He put a sharp hook at the end of His teaching on friendship that was radical. Whatever you ask! Well, what do we dare to ask? That the friends He's given us will know that He loves and forgives them? That He will bless and care for them?

Or do we claim that Christ can mysteriously and miraculously work in the depth of their natures to set them free of whatever bondage keeps them from wholeness in Him?

Over the years, but recently with new confidence, I have been led to pray for people at a much more profound level. Some people the Lord puts on my prayer agenda have such obvious personality needs that it's not difficult to know how to pray for their healing. Others require prolonged times of asking the Lord how to pray for the problems they are facing hidden beneath the surface. But, in either case, prayer in Jesus' name—that is, with His guidance on how to pray and with the assurance of the release of His power—results in His invasion of the deepest recesses of a person's nature. Christ sets the captives free when we pray in His name. No one is beyond the reach of His healing Spirit.

Intercessory prayer that asks for and expects miracles both in the personalities and the circumstances of our friends is the ultimate expression of faith in Christ's power and our love for them.

But this confidence must be renewed every day. Like that night when a young boy was used by the Lord to shock me with the realization that three people were burdens I was carrying rather than assignments from the Lord to love and pray for expecting His miracles. Since that night I've followed orders to communicate unqualified friendship. And in all three I've observed significant changes in their personalities. The healing Liberator is at work in them! The glory goes to Him and mine is the silent satisfaction watching Him do miracles. All because He's given me the privilege of being His friend and constantly calls me back into the adventure of seeking to be to others what He's been to me.

14

HANDLING FAILURES IN THE VICTORIOUS CHRISTIAN LIFE

IT WAS THE WAY the woman asked the question that bothered me. There was a note of self-righteousness coupled with glibness.

"Are you claiming, living, and preaching the victorious Christian life?" she asked.

The implication was that she was living a life of continuous victory and wanted to be assured I was too.

I asked, "What do you mean by victorious Christian life?"

"Oh, you know what I mean—a life without problems, one in which we just live victoriously for the Lord!"

"A life without any failure?" I asked.

"Absolutely!" she responded. "Christ is the victory!"

"Don't you ever do or say things that you realize later were less than the Lord's best for you?" I asked, hoping for some honesty.

The woman looked at me intently for a moment and then responded, "My task is to live the victorious Christian life for Christ." Then she said, "I concentrate on being victorious, not on the negative."

With that she swished off in a "victorious" flourish. She may have been afraid of any further questions. I suspected that there were some real needs and genuine failures in her life under her manikin-like smile.

A friend who had overheard my conversation came up and said, "Don't let that woman bother you—she's got real problems!"

What Is the Victorious Christian Life?

Some years ago, the phrase, "The victorious Christian life" found its way into our Christian vocabulary. It was biblical in both its roots and its intention. The emphasis was on Christ's power to bring victory out of life's most difficult problems. The popularizers of the phrase were authentic people who admitted their failures and claimed Christ's power for their needs.

But then a subtle shift took place. The emphasis on victory implied that Christians should always be victorious. The focus shifted from what Christ could do, to what we are to do to be victorious *for* Christ. The sin of pride reared its head. People's victories were touted as their own achievements. The bigger the victory the better. Acceptance in some circles was dependent on a continuous flow of these victories.

The tragedy was that people began to live a double life— a victorious exterior and an inner life of unmet needs. To whom could you admit your failures? Victory was the badge of success and the ticket to acceptance in the fellowship. Problems which were overcome were acceptable, but there could be no outward indication of unresolved problems. Often emotional problems, fears, guilts, negative attitudes, broken relationships which needed healing, resentments, angers, and jealousies were hidden beneath the highly polished surface of victorious Christian living.

The Tragic Result

The tragic result of hidden problems is severe judgmentalism about the failures of others. I'm convinced that often our severity is rooted in our own brand of hidden sin or our proclivity to some weakness. We are especially harsh on others who do what we've done and hidden, or do what we have been tempted to do.

Some preachers and teachers of the victorious life find themselves in this dilemma. If you proclaim that life can be victorious all of the time, what do you do with your inadequacies? Wouldn't exposure of faults reduce the effectiveness of a leader?

It is this attitude that starts what I call the camouflage syndrome. When leaders are not honest about their own needs, their followers can't admit theirs. And pretending to be more than we are keeps us from being vulnerable to experience the very victory Christ wants to give us in our problems. We build a facade and miss freedom in Christ.

Being Honest about Our Failures

I believe firmly in the victorious power of Christ in my life. That most certainly doesn't mean, though, that I am always victorious. Sometimes I fail in following the Lord's guidance and I fall short of measuring up to His best for my life. Who doesn't? These times become the opportunities of receiving Christ's victorious forgiveness and growing as a person.

Truth has to be constantly rediscovered to be reproduced. Often the week after preaching some biblical truth, I'm put through an experience in which I must live out what I preached. Or in the days prior to writing or speaking on Christ's power, I face difficulties in which what I am planning to say becomes deeply personal. Sharing that I'm still wrestling with a problem and seeking Christ's guidance is sometimes more helpful to people than just success stories. Both kinds of sharing are part of vulnerability. We dare not hide either Christ's victories or the areas where we need them.

Over a year ago, I experienced one of the most stressful weeks of my life. It also happened to be the same week that the author's copy of my book *Making Stress Work for You* arrived in the mail. My wife, Mary Jane, opened the package. With a smile in her voice she handed me the book and said, "Here's a super book on how to handle stress. You need it!" She was right. We both laughed. I believe everything I wrote in that book about stress. I also believe I have to rediscover what I wrote every day.

The truly victorious life is being free to admit our inadequacies and failures and turn them over to our Lord for the victory of His forgiveness and his strength to begin again. Learning how to handle the problem of failure is one of the most crucial discoveries in being a successful Christian. It is important to understand, though, that success is not the absence of failures, but knowing how to claim Christ's victory over them.

Jesus' Promise for Handling Failures

In the sixteenth chapter of John, Jesus was very honest with the disciples about the problems and persecution they would face. But He also told them about His forthcoming victory in the Cross and Resurrection and that He would be with them in all adversities. In response, the disciples declared their belief in Him, "Now we are sure that You know all things, and have no need that anyone should question You. By this we believe that You came forth from God" (John 16:30).

Do you sense a note of human confidence and bravado in that? Not unlike some of the self-generated misconstruing of the victorious Christian life by some of us today. Surely there must have been something wrong in the disciples' attitude and tone because of the way Jesus responded. He knew that they would be tested and that some of them would fail in doubt, denial, and desertion.

"Do you now believe?" He asked pointedly. "Indeed the hour is coming, yes, has now come, that you will be scattered, each to his own, and will leave Me alone. And yet I am not alone, because the Father is with Me" (vv. 31–32).

Instead of cheering their expression of belief, He told them how shallow it was and how quickly they would contradict it by their actions. He knew their hearts and wanted them to be able to deal with their subsequent failures. That's encouraging to us. Christ knows that our boldest statements of faith and firmest commitments of loyalty will not always be matched by our performance. That frees us to move beyond our great faith in the Lord, to faith in a great Lord! He wants to keep our attention on what He can do rather than on what we think we are able to do for Him.

I'm glad that John had the honesty to include this exchange between Jesus and the disciples. He had been there that night and had been a part of what happened. I'm also thankful that it took place because it prompted Jesus to give one of His most liberating promises—the promise of how He will help us handle our defeats, "These things I have spoken to you, that in Me you may have peace. In the world you will have tribulation; but be of good cheer, I have overcome the world" (v. 33).

Again we have a "these things I have spoken to you" reference to a previous teaching. That teaching had not only included His frank message about the suffering and persecution the disciples would face. But it also involved what He had just said about the failures which would follow their bold confession of belief. His promise in John 16:33 gives us a strategy for dealing with our failures which contradict our most ardent assurances of faithfulness and obedience.

The first part of Christ's promise is dependent on the second part. First, He promises peace and then He reveals what is the secret of experiencing that peace. "These things I have spoken to you that you may have peace." Peace in what? "In the world you will have tribulation." And how shall we handle the difficulties and failures in tribulation? "Be of good cheer, I have overcome the world."

This is one of those promises that needs to be looked at in reverse order. Often Jesus' most salient promises have the power punch line at the end, defining the enabling force for the first part of the statement. This is especially true of Christ's promise in John 16:33.

It is because Christ overcame and overcomes that we can face tribulation. We can experience the peace His overcoming presence provides. Let's look at that promise from that perspective as we attempt to discover its meaning for our weakness in times of difficulties.

Christ's Victorious Power

What did Jesus mean when He said, "I have overcome the world"? Some interpreters of this verse marvel that Jesus could say this even before the passion of Calvary and the Resurrection on Easter morning. But look more closely at the tense in the Greek text. "I have overcome" is in the perfect active indicative which is used for a present result of a past action. The basic verb is *nikaō,* which is related to the word *nikē,* "victory." Why did John use *nenikēka,* in the perfect tense? Because He knew that Jesus was referring to a previous victory which would be further expressed in the Cross. It was Jesus' commitment to do His Father's will that was the victory.

Jesus, as Son of God, revealed the purpose and power of God's will. As Son of Man, He was the first completely obedient man since the beginning of Creation. His victory was expressed in the words, "I came not to do My own will but the will of Him who sent Me" (John 5:30).

You remember that immediately following Jesus' baptism, He went alone into the wilderness of Judea where He was tempted by Satan. In that experience He won the battle to do the Father's will. In each confrontation with Satan's efforts to get Him to accomplish God's purposes by human manipulation, Jesus reaffirmed His commitment to obey God's will by God's power. And in confrontations with the leaders of Israel, He rejected their attempts to demean His calling as Messiah. When Peter tried to dissuade Jesus from the Cross and the other disciples tried to distract Him with their own ambitions for Him, He was resolute in His purpose. He had come to save the world. Nothing or no one could keep Him from the reason for which He was born. Long before that night preceding Calvary Jesus had settled the issue.

Overcoming the World

The word "world" was used in various ways in the New Testament. It represented the planet earth and all levels of life. Then it also meant a fallen humanity in opposition to, and in rebellion against, God. Further, the "world" signified the pervasive force of evil personified in Satan. Finally, it symbolized the spirit of human self-justification. At worst it was the human desire to be our own god; at best it is our own effort to be adequate before the Lord God on our own strength and religious perfectionism. The "world" was human pride.

Jesus said, "My kingdom is not of this world." He didn't mean that His kingdom was not present in the world, on earth, or that it could not be entered now. But He meant that His kingdom was completely contrary to the spirit of the world—the desire of humankind to control and run things by its own power. Christ's kingdom was centered in God's plan, directed by God's rule, and it required complete commitment to God's will.

The final phase of "overcoming" took place at Calvary. There He fought and conquered the spirit of the world, the spirit of evil, and the spirit of self-justification. In that cosmic, ultimate battle He won our forgiveness.

Christ's Victory and Ours

Christ's victory has profound implications for us as we face our day-to-day problems. His victory has reconciled us to God once and for all. In Him we are declared not guilty. But, in addition, Christ's victory has released tremendous power for us. We live now in the same world Jesus overcame. It is in this world that He told us we would have tribulation. The Greek word for tribulation is *thlipsis,* meaning "pressure or difficulties which rub us raw." We will experience that from the spirit of the world seeking to press us into its mold, demanding we do things its way and justifying ourselves by our effort. By tribulation, I think Christ not only meant life's difficulties, but our reaction to them. When we fail in handling difficulties, we are often tempted to try harder in our own strength or to grovel in self-condemnation.

Between this kind of tribulation and Christ's assurance that He has overcome the spirit of the world are His encouraging words, "Be of good cheer." The Greek word here is *tharseite,* from *tharseō,* meaning "to have courage." We are to be courageous, or more accurately, we are to take courage. Christ not only offers us the courage that comes when we remember He has won on Calvary, but He also gives us His own Spirit of courage for our particular needs. Our victory is to trust Him and not ourselves; His victory is to do for our problems exactly what He did on Calvary. The victorious Christian life is appropriating the once-for-all victory for our present and immediate problems.

This promise means everything to us in times when our problems cause the *thlipsis* kind of pressure of the world, and we are tempted to take things into our own hands and try to solve them on our own. When we fail, we have the alternative of remorse or receiving the rejuvenation of Christ's courage.

Now we can understand why Christ honestly told the disciples—and us—that we would know times of failure. He wanted to prepare us to trust Him and not our efforts at perfectionism,

"These things I have spoken to you, *that in Me* you may have peace" (italics mine). Peace is His special gift when we "take courage" and trust Him and not ourselves. It is the peace about which He had spoken earlier, "Peace I leave with you, My peace I give to you; not as the world gives do I give to you. Let not your heart be troubled, neither let it be afraid" (John 14:27).

At the conclusion of Communion services in our church the people turn to one another and say, "The peace of the Lord Jesus be with you." One day after Communion, Jim, a young executive who has recently become a Christian, asked me, "Exactly what are we doing when we give 'The Peace'? What is peace anyway?"

I suggested he think of the five fingers of his hand as he extended it to another person when offering the peace of Christ. "There are at least five aspects of the peace you are offering. They all start with '*p*' so it's easy to remember." I told Jim that peace comes from the *presence* of Christ. Peace is what He gives because it is what He is. Second, I told him that peace is the result of Christ's *pardon.* Peace is knowing that we are forgiven. Third, peace is the assurance of Christ's *provision*, His strength in our needs, given to us on time and in time in life's problems. There's no peace as long as we are constantly worrying about whether or not we're going to make it through difficulties. Fourth, peace is having a clear *purpose*, knowing that we have surrendered our lives to Christ and that He will guide us hour by hour in doing what He guides. And fifth, peace is the experience of Christ's *pleasure.* It is knowing that He loves us, that not even our mistakes can cause Him to stop loving us. Knowing that motivates us to live our lives to His glory. A part of that aspect of peace is knowing that He has defeated death, that through Him we are alive forever and can live now without fear.

Jim responded with enthusiasm. "Can't wait for the next communion!" he said with that wonderful openness of a new Christian.

A few weeks later I saw Jim at a service club we both belong to. As we sat down to lunch he offered me his hand. We already had shaken hands when we greeted each other. Jim beamed when he said, "Lloyd, the peace of the Lord Jesus be with you today. All five fingers of it!" He went on to share what had been happening to him since our talk after Communion that Sunday. He had told his wife about the five fingers of the hand of peace. They decided they both need all aspects of that peace renewed every day. So, in addition to their usual good-by hug before they both went off to their jobs, they would hold hands and assure each other of Christ's peace for the day.

Jim also began greeting the members of his Caring Cluster, a small group of Christian businessmen who meet with him once a week, with the same encouraging gift of peace when they met together.

"Most exciting of all," Jim said, "is thinking 'the peace' every time I shake hands with someone in my work! It makes all the difference in my attitudes. I hold warm, affirming thoughts for the person, thinking to myself, 'Christ loves you and wants you to know His peace.' And then I pray, 'Christ, if You want me to talk to this person about You, open up an opportunity so it's natural and authentic.' It's been amazing how many times I've been able to talk about my new faith these last few weeks. And when that doesn't happen, at least I know that my silent prayer for people will be answered. People are so pressured. They need Christ's peace.

"Something else," Jim went on with excitement, "in tough meetings when things get tense, I just slip my hand up on my head and say to myself, 'Peace, Jim, peace. Christ's peace!' Is that okay? If I can give peace to others, why not myself by claiming that Christ is with me?"

My response was filled with admiration for Jim's practical Christianity. "It's okay, Jim, all five fingers of it!"

We need the peace of Christ especially in times of failure. In every human failure there are three elements. What happened; how we react to what happened; and what we allow

Christ to give us to change our reaction to what happened. Usually, we brood over the failure, and then we condemn ourselves. We reach out for the peace the world gives, by attempting to handle the failure in our own strength. That usually leads to remorse and to justifying ourselves by explaining it away, or by blaming someone else or some other circumstances. On the other hand, the peace Christ offers is radically different. It is the peace that floods our hearts when we honestly acknowledge whatever part we've had in the failure. When we experience Christ's forgiveness, we can forgive ourselves. And out of that comes the freedom to forgive the people who may have caused the failure. Being a Christian doesn't mean we always have to take the blame. But it does mean that we must forgive. The sooner the better.

Failures bring us back to the death and the resurrection experience of profound peace. When we fail or must forgive someone whose failure has caused us pain, eventually we have to admit we can't handle it ourselves. That shatters our false pride. In a mysterious way that willful person inside us has to die so that the new person Christ wants to make us can live. I think that's a vital part of what it means to take up our cross. Our pride is crucified, we die to our own pride, and out of the ashes of whatever the failure was, we are raised up to a new beginning to live with the calm confidence of Christ's peace and the fear-dispelling strength of His courage. Then we can say with Paul, "I have been crucified with Christ; it is no longer I who live, but Christ lives in me; and the life which I now live in the flesh I live by faith in the Son of God, who loved me and gave Himself for me" (Gal. 2:20).

I talked to a father recently who had to claim that for his feelings of failure with his son. The son had dumped all of his frustrations on his dad blaming him for the mistakes he had made raising him. The father listened with Christ-inspired patience. He knew his son had to get it off his chest. After the encounter, however, he ached with a sense of failure. Had he really been that bad a father? He spent long hours

206 IF GOD CARES, WHY DO I STILL HAVE PROBLEMS?

in prayer asking the Lord for help to sort it all out. Yes, in many ways he had not met his son's needs. He confessed each memory. But then the Lord helped him remember all the good things he had done, and the creative influence he had been, in spite of his son's perception. After several days the father felt led to talk to his son again about the matter. He was very open with his son about what he had learned in his prayers. The son was impressed with his father's honesty. After a long time of sharing and tears, the father said, "Son, no one has had a perfect father. You'll know that soon enough when you become one. Mine wasn't perfect and, as we've both agreed, neither was yours. But now my concern is for you and helping you take responsibility for your own future."

The son's response after really thinking about that was, "I guess that's what I really wanted when I blasted you a couple of days ago. But, without our talk today, and all you've said, I wouldn't have heard you. Dad I really need your help right now. . . ."

The reason I found that so helpful was not only did it encourage me in my own role as a father but because it gave me a vivid, contemporary picture of what real victorious living is all about. The father in this account could have missed the chance of a lifetime with his son. Because he was open to allow Christ to deal with him and the past, he could be real with his son. That opened the son to take responsibility for his own future and be open to receive his dad's help— not because his dad was perfect, but because he now knew in a new way how much he loved him.

The Gift of Dynamic Faith

Now we are ready to press on to discover the power of the gift of faith in victorious living. The same John who recorded Jesus' promise about overcoming the world, gives us further help in understanding what that means in his first epistle. "For whatever is born of God overcomes the world.

And this is the victory that has overcome the world—our faith. Who is he who overcomes the world, but he who believes that Jesus is the Son of God?" (1 John 5:4–5). Now we see that the key to overcoming is faith. True faith is a gift, as we discussed earlier. The Lord gives us faith to accept His love and forgiveness. But it also enables us to claim what the Lord will do to help us with the problems we face. Faith leads us to pray for overcoming courage and then live with confidence to trust Him for the provision of supernatural resources.

The secret of receiving and expressing the gift of faith is in John's phrase "whatever is born of God overcomes the world." "Born of God" means that which comes from God, is generated by Him. Three things which come from God make possible an authentically victorious life. First, there must be a profound "rebirth" experience in us. We were "born again" when we committed our lives to the Lord. We started life anew with a totally fresh beginning. Second, as new people we discover that the Lord wants to give us His promises for our problems. When we claim the promise that He cares and will show us the way, we seek His guidance. He uses our imaginations to picture what it is that He wants to do in the problem confronting us. The vision is "born of God" in that it has been generated from His infinite wisdom of what is best for us. Third, we are given faith to trust that what He has revealed will be accomplished in His way and timing. Even when He chooses not to give us the whole picture all at once, He gives us courage to live with trust that He will give us enough direction to take one step at a time. This too is "born of God" because it is generated in us by His indwelling Spirit. So a defeat or failure or what seems to be an impossible challenge opens us up to the vision and the faith the Lord generates, allows to be born, in our minds and hearts. We never outgrow our need for that nor does life remain placid long enough to allow us to think we can make it on our own.

Some time ago, I was on an island during a hurricane. The

winds blew with ferocious force from one direction. Then, suddenly they ceased and there was a welcome calm. I remarked to a friend who lived there, "Well, I'm glad that's over!" In response he cautioned, "Not so! We're now in the calm of the eye of the hurricane. In a few minutes the winds will come back with the same force from the other direction." He was right. My confidence that the storm was over was ill-founded. It was only half over.

Life is like that. Perhaps you are enjoying one of those times of calm right now. You can't imagine you'd ever fail the Master again. But the winds will blow another day. Times will come when we'll fall back on our own strength to try to stand against the winds, or pick ourselves up and try to keep going by our grit. But the Lord offers us something much more powerful to brace for the storm. He gives us the calm of the eye of the hurricane to be our inner confidence when the winds beat on us again. It is then we will hear Him say what He said to the disciples during a storm on the Sea of Galilee, "Take courage, it is I." In the storm and in the calm we'll glorify Him for His peace.

With that assurance from the Lord we can face all the unresolved, hurting memories of the past and all the present unhealed brokenness inside and claim Christ's victorious power. Then we won't have to pretend outwardly that we're living the victorious Christian life while feeling defeated inside. We won't have to prove we're victorious. Christ alone will be our victory.

Who Gets the Glory?

I like the motto that hangs on the wall of a prayer room in a church in the Highlands of Scotland. It's a plaque with a quote on it from James Denny, the famous Scots teacher and theologian of another generation. "No man can at the same time prove that he is clever and that Christ is mighty to save." That's a good motto for victorious living.

So take courage! Christ has and will continue to win out over our present and future failures and problems. All He asks is that we give Him the glory. Then no one will gain the false impression we did it ourselves for Christ and fall into the trap of trying to deal with their problems by their own effort. Paul was on target when he wrote, "We have this treasure in earthen vessels, that the excellence of the power may be of God and not of us" (2 Cor. 4:7).

How do we then succeed when we've failed?

> Admit our failure—
> Acknowledge our feelings of self-condemnation
>   and self- justification—
> Accept Christ's victory on the cross—
> Ask Him for forgiving peace for the past,
>   vision of His plan, and strengthening
>   courage for the future—
> Press on!

15

BEYOND OUR DOUBTS AND BETTER THAN OUR DREAMS

AFTER I FINISHED a Good Friday message to The Los Angeles Rotary Club last spring, a man named Mike came up to talk with me.

"You really believe all that, don't you?" he said. "I used to be sure of what I believed, but I've got lots of doubts."

"So do I!" My response surprised him.

"Really?" he queried.

"Sure, we all have doubts. The issue is—are they standing between us and the Lord or pressing us to Him?"

"Well, that's a different twist," he exclaimed. "I used to be a member of a church, but they said it was a sin to doubt—so I left."

"Come to my church," I said, with a chuckle. "It's full of doubters!"

That really intrigued Mike. So I went on to explain that doubt is not bad. It's not unbelief, but the prelude to new belief. I shared that I firmly believed all that I had said in my talk that day about the Cross and the Resurrection, but that my doubts were in other areas where the Lord was pressing me to grow in my complete trust in Him.

"We are constantly challenged by new discoveries," I continued. "Often the edge of that growth is defined by our doubts. Whatever we are doubting shows us where we are in our development with the Lord. He is not put off by our doubts because He knows that means we are thinking and want to understand. Doubt is nothing more than the condition of mind and emotion that we experience before taking a new step in a growing faith."

"So you're saying that we will always have a next step, and that we'll probably experience this creative kind of doubt all through our lives?" Mike questioned.

"That's right! Now let's talk about *your* doubts, and I promise not to put you down for them," I said.

As it turned out, Mike was not the awful doubting sinner his former pastor had led him to think. Actually, all that Mike had ever confessed to him was that he had some troublesome doubts, but that was more than the pastor wanted to hear.

Instead of asking Mike what the doubts were about, he launched straight into a dissertation on the danger of ever doubting any aspect of the Christian faith. The impression he gave Mike was that he had to accept everything with no question. Especially no doubt!

The pastor had warned that Mike's doubts would be contagious and would unsettle his whole church. So Mike hadn't been back to church since that incredibly insensitive and fearful response he had received. He had closed the door on the church and finding answers to his questions.

Now Mike was again opening the door a crack by raising the subject of his doubts with me. His response to my message that day about Christ's living power and presence with us led me to suspect that his problem with doubt was really a question as to whether it's possible for us to have a personal relationship with the Lord today.

As I probed a bit, my impression was confirmed. Mike didn't doubt that Christ had lived on earth, or that He had died on the cross for our sins, or even that He had been raised from the dead. Rather, his real doubt was whether He has anything to do with our life today.

"It all seems so mysterious and unreal," Mike confided. "A personal relationship with Christ? How can you be so sure? You talk about Him as someone really alive, here and now— able to listen to you and willing to guide your life. Can that really happen?"

"It's an astounding assurance, isn't it?" I said, empathetically. "It hits me with full force everytime I face a really big problem and wonder, 'Can Christ do anything about this dilemma?' Everything seems against believing that He can and will intervene with exactly what I need, but He always does. Years of trusting Him have given me confidence that He will help me solve some problems immediately or give me courage to endure some others until the time for a solution is right."

The word "problems" and the idea of trusting Christ for His help seemed to really connect with Mike.

So I went on to share essentially what I have tried to communicate in this book. The reigning Christ—God with us—uses our problems for our growth and His glory. When He allows a problem to surface, it's because there's something He wants to accomplish in us and through us—something He wants to change, enable, or give that we wouldn't be open to receive unless the problems had pried open our minds and hearts to our need for Him. And the problems are only preludes to the miracles He will perform.

It was clear to me that, like all of us, Mike had problems. And his biggest problem was accepting Christ as Lord of his life. Mike was a hard-hitting realist for whom seeing was believing, and his seeing was clouded by his doubt that Christ could help him with his problems.

I'd worked with people like Mike before—thousands of

them. In fact, I'm drawn to the Mikes in the world who are so near and yet so far from a personal relationship with Christ. Churches are filled with them. I meet them wherever I go. Men and women, young and old, successful and not so successful. And they've all got unresolved problems.

But most of them are open to a first-step challenge to do an experiment with faith. I suggest a simple two-week trial period of trusting their biggest problem to Christ, asking for His intervention and help. Then I keep in close touch with them to share what's happening.

That kind of faith experiment seldom fails. The reason is that our Lord delights to take us where we are, but also to move us off dead center. He takes our problem seriously and responds to our least bit of openness to trust Him. He knows that the display of His power in solving the pressing problem at hand will prepare for a complete surrender of our whole life to Him.

This is where we pastors miss with the Mikes of this world. We present conceptual truths and ask for an intellectual response verbalized in the confession of Christ as Lord. Most don't know what that really means.

What they do know is that they face problems. Since the down-to-earth, gutsy ones are seldom talked about in Christian circles, they too seldom connect the Lordship of Christ with their daily needs. Relevance is missing. "Just accept Christ as Lord!" we admonish, without ever sharing what that really means for the big issues of our lives. Some comply and verbalize assent. We think we have helped them. Actually, all we've done is polish the surface while underneath are the same old problems.

But people like Mike won't put up with that. They turn off glib religious people and find many churches an anachronism.

Mike's biggest problem was that he was a "driven" man. A deep insecurity from childhood had pressed him to try to find his worth in success. Even when signs of that success had come his way, he could not relax and enjoy them. Every problem loomed up as a potential failure which would begin the landslide to an exposure of the inadequacy he felt inside.

All this came tumbling out as we stood there in the ballroom of the hotel where the Rotary Club meeting had been held. Others had left, the waiters had cleared all the tables, and Mike and I were all alone.

"Let's sit down and talk further," I suggested. Mike was ready to do that. We talked on into the afternoon about his lack of deep communication with his wife and his longing for a closeness with his children. Meanwhile, he was facing what he called an insurmountable problem at work which he thought could shipwreck his career.

A major account he had acquired for his company was in danger of being lost. Mike felt panicked and as a result was more a part of the growing problem than the source of leadership to solve it.

"Okay, Mike," I said, "why don't we pray right now and do a two-week experiment of faith with this problem? The Lord wants to show you He is present with you and can help you with it. I won't guarantee how He will do it, but be sure of this, you'll come through this problem convinced that He has been with you giving you strength and confidence and wisdom beyond your talent and skill. What's more, I think it will break the bind of your doubts about what He can do today in your life. All I'm asking you to do is commit this problem to Him now and pray every day for the next two weeks for His guidance and power."

There in the deserted ballroom, we prayed. I started off, praying for Mike and his need and asking the Lord not only to help solve his problem but to do it in a way that would set him free of his doubt about the Lord's present involvement in his life.

There was a long silence after I finished my prayer. I waited, praying on in silence that the Lord would give Mike the gift of faith and willingness to pray himself. Though the wait was only a brief time, it seemed like hours.

When Mike did pray, his words were honest, real, and from the depth of his heart. "Dear Christ, I've been moved today to entertain the thought that You're alive and here. I'd really like to be sure of that. Help me with my doubts and this gnawing fear of failure and that success won't last Right now, I'm in trouble at work. I need help. Lloyd tells me You are concerned and can step in to solve problems—even ones like mine. He's encouraged me to commit this problem to You. So that's what I'm doing right now. Help me. Amen."

Not a bad prayer for a man who had been classified as a doubter by others and himself!

The first days of the next two weeks were turbulent ones for Mike. Each time I called him, he updated me on what was happening. Yes, he was keeping up the faith experiment and no, the problem wasn't solved. But Mike was a determined, strong man of his word and kept the experiment going.

Near the end of the two-week experiment, Mike got a startling, mind-blowing insight about the account he was in danger of losing. As he pursued the insight, it developed into a whole new strategy which he had never thought of before. His superiors called it masterful. One even said, "Mike, that's inspired!" and Mike had smiled inside. He knew it was—not his, but the Lord's. "Doubting Mike" was on the way!

That kind of Christ-guided answer for a problem may seem old hat to those who have been seeing Him work for years, but for Mike it was a miracle.

It was just a beginning. In these past months Christ has been tackling other problems in Mike's life, and he's not only convinced of Christ's presence and power but he's made a complete surrender of his whole life to the Lord. When I catch his eye each Sunday morning in church, he smiles and nods an "It really works!" assurance.

You and I know that assurance will be deepened as new problems surface in the future. Mike will have doubts about what the Lord can do in each new problem. But those doubts will press him into a deeper relationship with the Lord rather than holding the Lord at arm's length.

Mike was a contemporary Thomas. And like Thomas, his honest desire to be sure Christ was alive was met by the Lord Himself.

We've given Thomas the nickname "Doubting Thomas" even though the Scriptures never refer to him with that constricting definition. What John's Gospel does tell us about him is that he wanted to be sure Christ was alive after the crucifixion.

Grief had gripped his soul as he had watched his beloved Master writhe on the cross. Exactly what he'd predicted when Jesus insisted on going to Jerusalem which was filled with His self-appointed enemies. But as Thomas watched Him die, something had died inside him also. Hope. What was left now without Jesus, the joy of being with Him, the vision of sharing His kingdom?

Fear gripped Thomas and he fled for safety after the crucifixion. He went into hiding all alone. He wanted to block out from his mind all the memories. In a self-imposed solitary confinement he nursed his grief—and his guilt. He had been a coward and had not helped the Master when He needed him. Now the King was dead. And Thomas was not about to let himself feel again those deep stirrings of loyalty and trust he'd given to Jesus.

That helps us to appreciate why Thomas reacted the way he did when the disciples found him and told him of the miracle of the Resurrection. Hidden away alone, he had missed the appearance of the resurrected Lord.

"We have seen the Lord!" the disciples said with breathless excitement. "He is alive, Thomas!"

Well, what would you have said? If grief and disappointment held you in the kind of bondage Thomas was experiencing, what would you have done?

Realistic and resolute Thomas said what I think I might

have said under those same circumstances. "Unless I see in His hands the print of the nails, and put my finger into the print of the nails, and put my hand into His side, I will not believe" (John 20:25). Once broken-hearted, it's difficult to hope—to love—again.

But the reborn excitement of the disciples would not be put off. They insisted that Thomas come back into the fellowship and wait with them for the Lord's next appearance. The significant thing is that Thomas's doubts motivated him to want to find out for himself.

I guess that's why I admire Thomas so much. He was not satisfied with a secondhand experience. The witness of the other disciples intrigued him, but he had to see for himself. Creative doubt, honestly admitted, does that for us. It's a step in our faith, not an end of it.

When we look at what happened when Christ appeared again to the disciples and to Thomas, we discover awesome truths about how our problem-utilizing, problem-solving Lord works.

Christ came just for Thomas! When He entered the Upper Room, He went to Thomas as if he were the only disciple there. He offered to meet Thomas's test. "Reach your finger here, and look at My hands; and reach your hand here, and put it into My side. Do not be unbelieving, but believing."

Thomas was astonished. The risen Lord had heard his demand for proof. His Master was not only alive, but He was everywhere and all-perceiving. He knew what Thomas had said, the anguish he had been through.

As the amazed disciple stood before the glory of His Lord, a wondrous gift of faith surged through him, breaking the bonds of doubt and filling him with uncontainable joy and conviction. And with that new faith, given to him by the Lord Himself, Thomas made the most sweeping and unreserved confession recorded in all of the Gospels. "My Lord and my God!"

Thomas, who had dared to doubt, now soared above the

understanding and faith of all the others. Jesus was Messiah, Lord, and sublimely God with us!

That's the ultimate conviction, and it's given to those of us who will not settle for secondhand faith but are open about our doubts, then doubt our doubts, and finally in communion with the risen Christ, know that He is God's creative and recreating power with us and in us.

The question we've raised and dared to look at honestly in this book—*If God Cares, Why Do I Still Have Problems?*—is an expression of a kind of doubt. The doubt is that the Lord has a creative purpose and redemptive power for our problems. The doubt recurs when really big problems hit us or we experience a build-up of problems, and that's the time when the doubt can drive us to the Lord or keep us from Him—when we need Him most of all.

Asking the question that is the title of this book is really an expression of Thomas's "Unless I see, touch, know for myself" longing for firsthand experience. In response, the Lord does for us what He did for the disciple. He comes to us with love and strength. He arranges circumstances. Changes situations. Opens other people's minds. Goes before us to show the way. More than we dreamed possible happens.

And the greater gift the Lord gives to us is wrapped up in the promise He spoke to Thomas. It is the promise that binds all the promises we've considered into one ultimate promise. "Thomas, because you have seen Me, you have believed. Blessed are those who have not seen and yet have believed."

That's the far superior and much more satisfying blessedness, lasting joy, given to us in our problems. What Paul prayed for the Ephesians happens to us. "The eyes of our understanding being enlightened," we come to know the Lord more profoundly and we behold Him as He does His miracles in and around us. We'd never know Him in the fullness of His grace and power, nor be made into His likeness, if we never had problems and had not accepted our calling to be co-partners with Him in turning problems into progress. He will not leave us—or the people we love—unfinished and incomplete. The Lord has plans for us!

So when problems hit and when doubt about the Lord's caring invades your mind, surrender everything to Him. Then get ready—blessings beyond your frustrating doubt and better than your fondest dreams are on the way!

More Problem-Solving Help
from Dr. Ogilvie

You will be helped and inspired by these other life-changing products featuring Lloyd John Ogilvie:

- The bestselling book *Making Stress Work for You*. Available in hardcover or Proven-Word quality paperback.

- A book discussion kit for *Making Stress Work for You*. Includes a leader's manual, Enabler's logbook, three audio cassettes, and a paperback copy of the book. Dr. Ogilvie shares his perspective and practical insights into the secrets of stress management.

- *Surviving in the Midst of Worry and Stress,* a Life-Lifter audio cassette probing the causes of worry and what we can do about it with God's help.

- A video cassette on *Surviving in the Midst of Worry and Stress.* For those wishing to avoid worry, ulcers, and tension headaches through scriptural guidelines.

For information on these products, contact your local Christian bookstore; write to Word Inc., P.O. Box 1790, Waco, TX 76796; or call toll-free in Texas 1-800-792-3210, outside Texas 1-800-433-3327.